The Constitution of the United States of America

MODERN EDITION

The Constitution of the United States of America

★ ★ ★

MODERN EDITION

Rearranged and Edited for Ease of Reading

GREENLEAF
BOOK GROUP PRESS

Published by Greenleaf Book Group Press
Austin, Texas
www.gbgpress.com

Distributed by Greenleaf Book Group

For ordering information or special discounts for bulk purchases, please contact Greenleaf Book Group at PO Box 91869, Austin, TX 78709, 512.891.6100.

Design and composition by AURAS Design of Silver Spring, Maryland
Cover design by Greenleaf Book Group
Cover image: ©Shutterstock/Kate Swan

Publisher's Cataloging-in-Publication data is available.

ISBN 13: 978-1-62634-208-8

Part of the Tree Neutral® program, which offsets the number of trees consumed in the production and printing of this book by taking proactive steps, such as planting trees in direct proportion to the number of trees used: www.treeneutral.com

Printed in the United States of America on acid-free paper

TreeNeutral®

15 16 17 18 19 20   10 9 8 7 6 5 4 3 2 1

First Edition

Other Edition(s):
eBook ISBN: 978-1-62634-207-1

To the Reader

THE MODERN EDITION IS DESIGNED TO HELP YOU to read the United States Constitution with ease and understanding.

The Constitution is the oldest written national constitution in the world. Its original language of 1787 still provides the framework of government by which the nation meets each new challenge, while numerous amendments protect Americans' basic freedoms and their right to vote.

But the document is showing its age. It has grown ever more difficult to read, as a result of more than two centuries of change in its meaning and in the written English language. The logical organization of the original document has been lost as some provisions near the beginning have been modified by amendments placed toward the end. The eloquent language of the original is clouded for modern readers by its antiquated stylistic features—spelling, capitalization, punctuation, grammatical forms.

THE MODERN EDITION MAKES THE CONSTITUTION EASILY READABLE AGAIN, without any loss of accuracy. The text has been rearranged to present the current meaning of the Constitution in a clear and logical sequence:

- Provisions that are no longer effective have been moved to the back of the document, where they appear as "The Constitution of the Past."

- Procedural items that have served their purposes, such as time limits on the adoption of some amendments, have been moved to the very end of the Constitution.

- The amendments have been moved forward to the places where their subjects are dealt with in the original text, and to two new subdivisions on "Citizenship and the Right to Vote" and "Rights and Equality."

- A few changes have been made in the organization of the original Constitution, especially to distinguish the powers of the national government from the procedures and powers of its three branches.

The text has also been carefully edited, following today's rules of English usage, to modernize the features of the Constitution that have made it hard to read:

- Eighteenth-century spellings have been updated and the heavy use of capital letters has been abandoned.

- Excessive and confusing punctuation has been simplified and revised to help convey the meaning of long and complicated sentences; some such sentences have been divided for clarity by a small paragraph break or "phrase break."

- A few old-fashioned grammatical forms such as subjunctives have been replaced by their modern equivalents.

The Modern Edition provides some other aids for you, all designed to make the Constitution easier to read and study:

- Headings tell what each part of the text is about, while a detailed table of contents, composed of the major headings, enables the reader to see at a glance the Constitution in broad outline.

- The smallest units of text, called clauses, are numbered consecutively in each chapter for easy reference.

- Notations show the source of each of the Modern Edition's clauses in the original Constitution or the amendments.

Some printings of the Modern Edition, including this one, provide additional assistance:

- Definitions are given for many words and phrases that may be unfamiliar to some readers, as well as some that are used with special meanings in the Constitution. Pronunciations of words are given where needed.

- Footnotes explain a few matters on which the constitutional text may give a misleading expectation; they also tell how some parts of the text have become obsolete.

- An appendix shows the locations of the Bill of Rights and the later amendments in the Modern Edition; another gives a brief explanation of the Constitution's two typographical errors, corrected in the Modern Edition.

- An index gives the locations of all of the Constitution's important terms.

THE IMPROVED READABILITY OF THE MODERN EDITION has been achieved without harm to the Constitution's often-praised eloquence. The majestic language of the Founding Fathers has not been simplified or paraphrased; it has only been modernized in the few cases where it departs sharply from current usage.

The editorial improvements have likewise done no harm to the accuracy of the text. None of the changes affect the meaning of the Constitution, as revealed by its language and the Supreme Court decisions and political usages that have interpreted and applied it, except to make the meaning more clear.

While the Modern Edition focuses attention on today's Constitution, it can also aid the historical study of the document. In "The Constitution of the Past," the repealed and obsolete provisions are sorted into groups showing major stages, crises, and problems in the nation's history: the procedures for starting the new government after adoption of the Constitution, the establishment of slavery in the supreme law of the land, the adoption and repeal of Prohibition, and others. The historical forces and events that have made some clauses obsolete are explained by footnotes.

The Modern Edition provides, for the first time in two centuries, the text of the Constitution in a form that is well organized and free of antiquated literary and typographical features. This edition makes the study of the Constitution less difficult and more rewarding for students, citizens—everyone.

YOUR STUDY OF THE CONSTITUTION WILL BE EASIER if you notice how the Modern Edition is organized. It has nine major subdivisions called chapters.

Chapter 1 introduces the three branches of the national government: Congress, the executive, and the courts. It describes the ways in which the occupants of these offices are chosen; lays down the rules about their qualifications, terms, and pay; and provides for filling vacancies.

This chapter next establishes the procedures to be followed by the three branches and the powers to be exercised by them, separately or in cooperation, in making the laws and conducting the business of government.

Chapter 2 states the powers of the national government: legislative powers such as taxation and the regulation of interstate commerce, executive powers such as enforcement of the laws and command of the armed forces, and the judicial power to decide various kinds of legal cases.

Chapter 3 deals with the states, setting forth some duties that the national government owes to them, a few duties of each state to the others, and several limitations on the states.

Chapter 4 covers citizenship and the principal right that is limited to citizens: the right to vote.

Chapter 5 contains the limitations on governmental action that protect other rights. The rights that are protected against both the national and the state governments are listed first, followed by those that are only protected against the national government, then those protected only against the states.

Chapter 6 is about the Constitution itself: procedures for amending it, oaths to support it, and the supremacy of the Constitution and the laws and treaties made under it.

Chapter 7, "The Constitution of the Past," shows the provisions that have been repealed or replaced, or have otherwise lost all force. (These can still be useful by helping us to understand the thinking of the document's authors.)

Finally, *Chapter 8* shows special procedures that were prescribed for adoption of the original Constitution and a few of the amendments, while *Chapter 9* shows the forms of the documents that proposed the original and many of the amendments, produced by the Constitutional Convention in 1787 and by Congress at later times.

You can gain a good understanding of today's Constitution by simply reading the Modern Edition from the Preamble to the end of Chapter 6. If you are interested in the history of the document you can go on to Chapters 7 to 9.

You can make a focused study of any subject that interests you (such as election of the President or the right to vote) by consulting the tables of contents or index and turning to the pages that contain the relevant provisions.

IN THIS BOOK, THE MODERN EDITION IS FOLLOWED by a copy of the original Constitution and the amendments in their original printed form. You will find this Traditional Arrangement useful when, in reading about the Constitution in other publications, you come across references to particular articles and amendments, and need to know exactly what these say.

AS YOU READ THE MODERN EDITION OF THE CONSTITUTION you are taking an important step toward an understanding of the government of the United States of America—the powers and procedures of government and the rights and freedoms of the people—in the twenty-first century.

—Henry Bain, Editor

Brief Contents

Detailed Contents

THE TRADITIONAL ARRANGEMENT OF THE CONSTITUTION

APPENDIXES

INDEX

THE MODERN EDITION
OF THE CONSTITUTION

The Constitution appears in the left-hand columns. The headings, definitions, footnotes, and other aids have been provided by the editor–they are not part of the adopted Constitution.

HEADINGS

The text of the Modern Edition is organized at five levels. At each level, a heading in a distinctive typeface tells what the subject is. Here are examples:

Chapter
Powers of the National Government

Division
Legislative Powers

Subdivisions
Finance

Raising Revenue

Power to Tax Incomes

Readers do not need to remember the levels or the typefaces. Their only purpose is to reveal the organization of the Constitution — to show what comes under what in the hierarchy of paragraphs, sentences, and phrases.

CLAUSES

The smallest units of text (the clauses) are numbered consecutively in each chapter. The number of each clause appears below it. Beside the number is a notation showing the source of the clause in an article of the original Constitution or an amendment.

DEFINITIONS

On the right side of each page are definitions of any words or phrases that may be unfamiliar to some readers or that are used with a special meaning. Each definition is located opposite the term's first appearance in the text.

A definition is labeled "as used here" if the word is used with a meaning that differs from ordinary modern usage, or if it is used with more than one meaning in the Constitution. A few definitions are qualified with a "perhaps," indicating that the precise meaning of the language is still uncertain.

PRONUNCIATIONS

The pronunciations of a few difficult words are shown in the definitions by respelling and stress marks. These words should be pronounced the way they look. In the respellings, ə stands for the indefinite vowel sound of an unstressed syllable, such as the *a* in alone and the *i* in recipe.

FOOTNOTES

At the bottoms of some pages are footnotes that explain a few constitutional phrases whose words may give a misleading impression. Footnotes in Chapter 7 tell how some provisions have become obsolete.

Preamble

Purposes of the Constitution, Adoption by the People of the United States

We, the people of the United States,

in order to form a more perfect union, establish justice, insure domestic tranquillity, provide for the common defense, promote the general welfare, and secure the blessings of liberty to ourselves and our posterity,

do ordain and establish this Constitution for the United States of America.

P.1 | PREAMBLE

preamble opening statement, introduction

domestic tranquillity peace and calm within the country, freedom from disturbance or rebellion

welfare well-being

posterity descendants

ordain enact, establish

Chapter 1
Organization and Operation
of the National Government

The Congress
Legislative Powers

All legislative powers herein granted shall be vested in a Congress of the United States, which shall consist of a Senate and House of Representatives.

1.1 | ART 1 SEC 1

legislative lawmaking

herein in this

shall be are and must be (as used here and in many places in the Constitution)

vested in placed in, given to

The House of Representatives
Term, Election

The House of Representatives shall be composed of members chosen every second year by the people of the several states, and the electors in each state shall have the qualifications requisite for electors of the state legislature.

1.2 | ART 1 SEC 2 CL 1

electors (of) voters (for) (as used here)

requisite (rek′wizit) **for** required of

Apportionment of Representatives Among the States, Census

Representatives shall be apportioned among the several states according to their respective numbers, but each state shall have at least one representative.

apportioned among the several states according to their respective numbers distributed among the states in proportion to their populations

The actual enumeration shall be made within every term of ten years, in such manner as the Congress shall by law direct.

enumeration census, population count

within every term of every

1.3 | 14TH AMEND SEC 2 & ART 1 SEC 2 CL 3

Qualifications

No person shall be a representative who shall not have attained the age of twenty-five years and been seven years a citizen of the United States, and who shall not, when elected, be an inhabitant of that state in which he shall be chosen.

attained reached

be an inhabitant of live in (as used here)

he he or she

1.4 | ART 1 SEC 2 CL 2

Filling Vacancies

When vacancies happen in the representation from any state, the executive authority thereof shall issue writs of election to fill such vacancies.

executive authority governor

thereof of it

writ of election an order for the conduct of an election

1.5 | ART 1 SEC 2 CL 4

Officers

The House of Representatives shall choose its speaker and other officers.

speaker presiding officer (as used here)

1.6 | ART 1 SEC 2 CL 5

The Senate

Term, Election, Equal Representation of the States

The Senate of the United States shall be composed of two senators from each state, elected by the people thereof for six years, and each senator shall have one vote. The electors in each state shall have the qualifications requisite for electors of the state legislature.

1.7 | 17TH AMEND

Overlapping Terms

The senators shall be divided as equally as may be into three classes, so that one-third may be chosen every second year.

1.8 | ART 1 SEC 3 CL 2

Qualifications

No person shall be a senator who shall not have attained the age of thirty years and been nine years a citizen of the United States, and who shall not, when elected, be an inhabitant of that state for which he shall be chosen.

1.9 | ART 1 SEC 3 CL 3

Filling Vacancies

When vacancies happen in the representation of any state in the Senate, the executive authority of such state shall issue writs of election to fill such vacancies.

The legislature of any state may empower the executive thereof to make temporary appointments, until the people fill the vacancies by election as the legislature may direct.

1.10 | 17TH AMEND

The Vice President Is President of the Senate

The Vice President of the United States shall be president of the Senate, but shall have no vote unless the senators are equally divided.

president presiding officer (as used here)

1.11 | ART 1 SEC 3 CL 4

Other Officers

The Senate shall choose its other officers, and also a president pro tempore* in the absence of the Vice President or when he shall exercise the office of President of the United States.

pro tempore (proh tem′pəree) for the time being, temporary

exercise perform (as used here)

1.12 | ART 1 SEC 3 CL 5

---

* Despite the title, the president pro tempore is usually elected to serve for a full two-year Congress.

Members of Congress

Election Procedures

The times, places, and manner of holding elections for senators and representatives shall be prescribed in each state by the legislature thereof, but the Congress may at any time by law make or alter such regulations.

1.13 | ART 1 SEC 4 CL 1

Terms Begin on January 3

The terms of senators and representatives shall end at noon on the third day of January, and the terms of their successors shall then begin.

1.14 | 20TH AMEND SEC 1

third day of January January 3 in odd-numbered years (as used here)

Compensation, Waiting Period for a Change in Compensation

The senators and representatives shall receive a compensation for their services, to be ascertained by law and paid out of the treasury of the United States, but

no law varying the compensation for the services of the senators and representatives shall take effect until an election of representatives shall have intervened.

1.15 | ART 1 SEC 6 CL 1 & 27TH AMEND

compensation salary, pay

ascertained (as′ər taynd″) prescribed, determined

the United States the national government (as used here and in many places throughout the document). The Constitution also sometimes uses "the United States" in a different sense, in referring to the nation, its territory, and its people or citizens (as in the Preamble and Clauses 1.4 and 1.9).

varying changing

intervene come between (that is, come between the law's passage and its taking effect)

Restrictions on Holding Other Offices

No person holding any office under the United States shall be a member of either house during his continuance in office,* and

under the United States in the national government

---

* Officers of the armed forces reserves have served as members of Congress.

no senator or representative shall, during the time for which he was elected, be appointed to any civil office under the authority of the United States which shall have been created, or the emoluments whereof shall have been increased, during such time.[*]

civil not military

emolument compensation, salary, fee

whereof of which

1.16 | ART 1 SEC 6 CL 2

Privilege of Speech or Debate

For any speech or debate in either house, the senators and representatives shall not be questioned in any other place.

questioned in any other place prosecuted or sued in any court, or called to account by any other part of the government

1.17 | ART 1 SEC 6 CL 1

Privilege from Arrest in Noncriminal Cases

They shall in all cases except treason, felony, and breach of the peace be privileged from arrest during their attendance at the sessions of their respective houses, and in going to and returning from the same.[†]

treason making war against one's nation, or helping its enemies

felony a serious crime

breach of the peace any lesser crime (as used here)

privileged exempt, immune

session a year's meetings and other business of Congress

1.18 | ART 1 SEC 6 CL 1

The President and Vice President

The Executive Power

The executive power shall be vested in a President of the United States of America.

executive putting into effect and enforcing the laws and the decisions of the courts; directing and administering the departments and offices of government

1.19 | ART 2 SEC 1 CL 1

---

[*] A few members of Congress have resigned in order to accept appointment, during the term for which they were elected, to an office whose salary had been increased during that term. Their salary has been limited, during their service in that office, to the amount that had been in effect before the increase.

[†] Arrests in noncriminal cases are now rare, but they can happen in a few kinds of such cases.

The President

Term, Qualifications

The President shall hold his office during the term of four years.

No person except a natural born citizen of the United States shall be eligible to the office of President; neither shall any person be eligible to that office who shall not have attained the age of thirty-five years and been fourteen years a resident within the United States.

1.20 | ART 2 SEC 1 CLS 1 & 5

natural born citizen a person born in this country, or born abroad to a parent or parents who are citizens

eligible (el′ i jə bl) qualified for selection

Two-Term Limit

No person shall be elected to the office of President more than twice, and

no person who has held the office of President, or acted as President, for more than two years of a term to which some other person was elected President shall be elected to the office of President more than once.

1.21 | 22ND AMEND SEC 1

The Vice President

The Vice President shall be chosen for the same term as the President.

No person constitutionally ineligible to the office of President shall be eligible to that of Vice President of the United States.

1.22 | ART 2 SEC 1 CL 1 & 12TH AMEND

Election of the President and Vice President

The President, together with the Vice President, shall be elected as follows:

1.23 | ART 2 SEC 1 CL 1

The Electoral Votes
The Electors

Each state shall appoint, in such manner as the legislature thereof may direct, a number of electors equal to the whole number of senators and representatives to which the state may be entitled in the Congress, but

appoint choose, elect (as used here)

elector a person chosen for the sole purpose of casting a vote for President and a vote for Vice President (as used here)

no senator or representative or person holding an office of trust or profit under the United States shall be appointed an elector.

office of trust or profit any office except one that is purely honorary

1.24 | ART 2 SEC 1 CL 2

Electors for the District of Columbia

The district constituting the seat of government of the United States shall appoint, in such manner as the Congress may direct, a number of electors of President and Vice President equal to the whole number of senators and representatives in Congress to which the district would be entitled if it were a state, but in no event more than the least populous state;

constituting being, serving as

seat of government capital city

the least populous state the state with the smallest population

they shall be in addition to those appointed by the states, but they shall be considered, for the purposes of the election of President and Vice President, to be electors appointed by a state, and they shall meet in the district and perform their duties as provided by the next clause.

The Congress shall have power to enforce this clause by appropriate legislation.

1.25 | 23RD AMEND

Voting by the Electors for President and Vice President, Transmitting the Results

The electors shall meet in their respective states and vote by ballot for President and Vice President, one of whom, at least, shall not be an inhabitant of the same state as themselves; they shall name in their ballots the person voted for as President and in distinct ballots the person voted for as Vice President, and

be an inhabitant of the same state assert one's presence in the state, as by registering to vote

they shall make distinct lists of all persons voted for as President and of all persons voted for as Vice President, and of the number of votes for each, which lists they shall sign and certify, and transmit sealed to the seat of the government of the United States, directed to the president of the Senate.

1.26 | 12TH AMEND

Times of Voting

The Congress may determine the time of choosing the electors and the day on which they shall give their votes, which day shall be the same throughout the United States.

give cast (as used here)

1.27 | ART 2 SEC 1 CL 4

Counting the Electoral Votes in Congress

The president of the Senate shall, in the presence of the Senate and House of Representatives, open all the certificates, and the votes shall then be counted.

1.28 | 12TH AMEND

Election of the President
The Person Having a Majority of Electoral Votes for President Becomes President

The person having the greatest number of votes for President shall be the President, if such number is a majority of the whole number of electors appointed.

a majority more than half

1.29 | 12TH AMEND

If No Person Has a Majority, the House of Representatives Chooses a President

If no person has such majority, then from the persons having the highest numbers, not exceeding three, on the list of those voted for as President, the House of Representatives shall choose immediately, by ballot, the President. But

not exceeding three not exceeding three persons

in choosing the President the votes shall be taken by states, the representation from each state having one vote; a quorum for this purpose shall consist of a member or members from two-thirds of the states, and a majority of all the states shall be necessary to a choice.

1.30 | 12TH AMEND

quorum the minimum number of members that must be present in order to do business

a choice the election of a President (as used here)

Election of the Vice President
The Person Having a Majority of Electoral Votes for Vice President Becomes Vice President

The person having the greatest number of votes for Vice President shall be the Vice President, if such number is a majority of the whole number of electors appointed.

1.31 | 12TH AMEND

If No Person Has a Majority, the Senate Chooses a Vice President

If no person has a majority, then from the two highest numbers on the list the Senate shall choose the Vice President; a quorum for the purpose shall consist of two-thirds of the whole number of senators, and a majority of the whole number shall be necessary to a choice.

1.32 | 12TH AMEND

the two highest numbers the two persons having the largest numbers of votes

Procedures in Case of the Death of a Candidate or President-elect, or Failure of a President to Take Office
Providing for the Case When No Candidate Has a Majority and a Candidate Dies

The Congress may by law* provide for the case of the death of any of the persons from whom the House of Representatives may choose a President whenever the right of choice shall have devolved upon it, and for the case of the death of any of the persons from whom the Senate may choose a Vice President whenever the right of choice shall have devolved upon it.

1.33 | 20TH AMEND SEC 4

devolved upon it passed on to it

* No such law has been enacted.

If a President Has Not Been Elected and Taken Office When the Term Begins, the Vice-President-elect Acts As President

If a President shall not have been chosen before the time fixed for the beginning of his term, or if the President-elect shall have failed to qualify, then the Vice-President-elect shall act as President until a President shall have qualified.

1.34 | 20TH AMEND SEC 3

President-elect a person who has been elected President by vote of the electors (or the House of Representatives) but has not yet taken office

qualify possess the qualifications for the office and take the oath of office

If the President-elect Has Died, the Vice-President-elect Becomes President

If, at the time fixed for the beginning of the term of the President, the President-elect shall have died, the Vice-President-elect shall become President.

1.35 | 20TH AMEND SEC 3

Providing for an Acting President When Neither a President nor a Vice President Takes Office

The Congress may by law provide for the case wherein neither a President-elect nor a Vice-President-elect shall have qualified, declaring who shall then act as President or the manner in which one who is to act shall be selected, and

wherein in which

such person shall act accordingly until a President or Vice President shall have qualified.

1.36 | 20TH AMEND SEC 3

Filling Vacancies

The Vice President Succeeds the President

In case of the removal of the President from office or of his death or resignation, the Vice President shall become President.

1.37 | 25TH AMEND SEC 1

Filling a Vacancy in the Vice Presidency

Whenever there is a vacancy in the office of Vice President, the President shall nominate a Vice President who shall take office upon confirmation by a majority vote of both houses of Congress.

1.38 | 25TH AMEND SEC 2

nominate propose someone to be appointed or elected to an office

confirmation approval

Providing for an Acting President
When Both the President and Vice President
Have Left Their Offices Vacant or Are Disabled

The Congress may by law provide for the case of removal, death, resignation, or inability both of the President and Vice President, declaring what officer shall then act as President, and

such officer shall act accordingly until the disability is removed or a President is elected.

1.39 | ART 2 SEC 1 CL 6

Disability of the President

When the President Declares Inability
to Perform the Office, the Vice President
Becomes Acting President

Whenever the President transmits to the president pro tempore of the Senate and the speaker of the House of Representatives his written declaration that he is unable to discharge the powers and duties of his office, and until he transmits to them a written declaration to the contrary,

discharge exercise, perform

such powers and duties shall be discharged by the Vice President as Acting President.

1.40 | 25TH AMEND SEC 3

When the President Is Declared to Be Disabled

Whenever the Vice President and a majority of either the principal officers of the executive departments, or of such other body as Congress may by law provide,* transmit to the president pro tempore of the Senate and the speaker of the House of Representatives their written declaration that the President is unable to discharge the powers and duties of his office,

1.41 | 25TH AMEND SEC 4

the principal officers of the executive departments the heads (secretaries) of the departments of the national government. They, with a few other top officials, are members of the President's cabinet.

the Vice President Becomes Acting President

the Vice President shall immediately assume the powers and duties of the office as Acting President.

1.42 | 25TH AMEND SEC 4

assume take on, take over

If the President Thereafter Declares That No Inability Exists, the President Resumes the Office

Thereafter, when the President transmits to the president pro tempore of the Senate and the speaker of the House of Representatives his written declaration that no inability exists, he shall resume the powers and duties of his office

1.43 | 25TH AMEND SEC 4

thereafter after that

resume take back

unless the President Is Again Declared to Be Disabled

unless the Vice President and a majority of either the principal officers of the executive departments, or of such other body as Congress may by law provide, transmit within four days to the president pro tempore of the Senate and the speaker of the House of Representatives their written declaration that the President is unable to discharge the powers and duties of his office.

1.44 | 25TH AMEND SEC 4

---

* No other body has been provided.

*Then Congress Decides
Whether the President Is Disabled*

Thereupon Congress shall decide the issue, assembling within forty-eight hours for that purpose if not in session.

thereupon then, immediately after that

If the Congress, within twenty-one days after receipt of the latter written declaration or, if Congress is not in session, within twenty-one days after Congress is required to assemble, determines by two-thirds vote of both houses that the President is unable to discharge the powers and duties of his office,

the Vice President shall continue to discharge the same as Acting President;

otherwise, the President shall resume the powers and duties of his office.

1.45 | 25TH AMEND SEC 4

Beginning of Terms, Compensation

Terms Begin on January 20

The terms of the President and Vice President shall end at noon on the twentieth day of January, and the terms of their successors shall then begin.

twentieth day of January January 20 in each odd-numbered year following a year whose number is evenly divisible by four

1.46 | 20TH AMEND SEC 1

Compensation

The President shall at stated times receive for his services a compensation which shall neither be increased nor diminished during the period for which he shall have been elected, and he shall not receive within that period any other emolument from the United States or any state.

1.47 | ART 2 SEC 1 CL 7

The Courts
The Judicial Power

The judicial power of the United States shall be vested in one Supreme Court and in such inferior courts as the Congress may from time to time ordain and establish.

1.48 | ART 3 SEC 1

judicial judging; hearing and deciding cases and controversies; conducting the business of the courts of law

inferior lower

Term and Compensation of Judges

The judges, both of the supreme and inferior courts, shall hold their offices during good behavior, and shall at stated times receive for their services a compensation which shall not be diminished during their continuance in office.*

1.49 | ART 3 SEC 1

during good behavior until they die, choose to retire, resign, or are removed by impeachment and conviction as provided in Clauses 1.74–1.77

Procedures of the Three Branches of Government
The Congress
Time of Assembling

The Congress shall assemble at least once in every year, and such meeting shall begin at noon on the third day of January unless the Congress shall by law appoint a different day.

1.50 | 20TH AMEND SEC 2

Limitations on Adjournment

Neither house during the session of Congress shall, without the consent of the other, adjourn for more than three days, nor to any other place than that in which the two houses shall be sitting.

1.51 | ART 1 SEC 5 CL 4

adjourn stop doing business and depart (after setting the time and place of the next meeting)

place city (as used here)

---

* This clause applies to the Supreme Court and to all courts established by exercise (use) of the power given in Clause 1.48. It does not apply to a few specialized courts established by exercise of powers given in Clause 1.73 or other clauses, such as the courts for bankruptcy cases (Clause 2.12) and territories (Clause 2.29).

Judging the Elections and Qualifications of Members

Each house shall be the judge of the elections, returns, and qualifications of its own members.

1.52 | ART 1 SEC 5 CL 1

returns official reports of election results

judge of the . . . qualifications judge of whether persons elected to Congress possess the qualifications established by the Constitution

Rules, Discipline, Removal from Office

Each house may determine the rules of its proceedings, punish its members for disorderly behavior, and with the concurrence of two-thirds, expel a member.

1.53 | ART 1 SEC 5 CL 2

concurrence agreement

expel eject, remove from office

Quorums, Compelling Attendance

A majority of each house shall constitute a quorum to do business, but a smaller number may adjourn from day to day and may be authorized to compel the attendance of absent members, in such manner and under such penalties as each house may provide.

1.54 | ART 1 SEC 5 CL 1

adjourn from day to day meet and conduct no business, but agree to meet again on one of the next few days

Journals, Recording of Votes

Each house shall keep a journal of its proceedings and from time to time publish the same, except such parts as may in its judgment require secrecy, and

the yeas and nays of the members of either house on any question shall, at the desire of one-fifth of those present, be entered on the journal.

1.55 | ART 1 SEC 5 CL 3

journal of its proceedings a record of the matters considered by the house, and its votes and actions, published after each annual session ends. The journal does not include the debates, which appear in the daily *Congressional Record*.

the yeas and nays the votes for and against

Revenue Bills

All bills for raising revenue shall originate in the House of Representatives, but the Senate may propose or concur with amendments as on other bills.

1.56 | ART 1 SEC 7 CL 1

bill a proposed law

raising revenue obtaining the money needed to meet the expenses of the government

concur agree

The Congress and the President

Convening and Adjourning Congress

The President may on extraordinary occasions convene both houses or either of them, and

convene both houses call on both houses to assemble

in case of disagreement between them with respect to the time of adjournment, he may adjourn them to such time as he shall think proper.

1.57 | ART 2 SEC 3

adjourn them order them to stop doing business and depart; also set the time of their next meeting (if there is to be another meeting before the next January 3)

Presidential Messages to Congress

He shall from time to time give to the Congress information on the state of the union and recommend to its consideration such measures as he shall judge necessary and expedient.

1.58 | ART 2 SEC 3

expedient producing a desired result, suitable and proper

Making Laws
Presentation of Bills to the President for Approval

Every bill which shall have passed the House of Representatives and the Senate shall, before it becomes a law, be presented to the President of the United States. If he approves, he shall sign it, but

1.59 | ART 1 SEC 7 CL 2

Procedure When the President Does Not Approve a Bill

if not, he shall return it with his objections to that house in which it shall have originated, which shall enter the objections at large on the journal and proceed to reconsider it.

at large in full, completely

If, after such reconsideration, two-thirds of that house shall agree to pass the bill, it shall be sent together with the objections to the other house, by which it shall likewise be reconsidered, and if approved by two-thirds of that house it shall become a law, but in all such cases the votes of both houses shall be determined by yeas and nays, and the names of the persons voting for and against the bill shall be entered on the journal of each house.

1.60 | ART 1 SEC 7 CL 2

*Outcome When the President
Does Not Sign or Return a Bill*

If any bill shall not be returned by the President within ten days (Sundays excepted) after it shall have been presented to him, the same shall be a law in like manner as if he had signed it, unless the Congress by adjournment prevents its return, in which case it shall not be a law.

1.61 | ART 1 SEC 7 CL 2

like the same

adjournment the final departure of Congress near the end of the two-year term for which representatives are elected, and (perhaps) its departure at the end of the first year's session, or for a vacation of more than a few days during a session (as used here)

Approval of Other Actions
of Congress by the President

Every order, resolution, or vote to which the concurrence of the Senate and House of Representatives may be necessary (except on a question of adjournment) shall be presented to the President of the United States, and before the same shall take effect shall be approved by him, or

being disapproved by him, shall be repassed by two-thirds of the Senate and House of Representatives, according to the rules and limitations prescribed in the case of a bill.*

1.62 | ART 1 SEC 7 CL 3

---

* Actions of the two houses approved in accordance with this clause, called joint resolutions, have the force of law.

The two houses of Congress pass some resolutions that are necessary in the conduct of their business, called concurrent resolutions, without presenting these to the President for approval. Examples are resolutions scheduling a joint session of the two houses, correcting an error in a printed bill, or stating an opinion or purpose of the two houses.

A resolution by which the two houses propose an amendment to the Constitution (called a joint resolution) is ordinarily not presented to the President, since that officer's approval is not required (see Clauses 6.1 and 6.2).

Making Treaties

The President shall have power, by and with the advice and consent of the Senate, to make treaties, if two-thirds of the senators present concur.*

1.63 | ART 2 SEC 2 CL 2

advice and consent approval

Appointments
Nomination by the President, Approval by the Senate

The President shall nominate, and by and with the advice and consent of the Senate shall appoint, ambassadors, other public ministers and consuls, judges of the Supreme Court, and all other officers of the United States whose appointments are not herein otherwise provided for, and which shall be established by law.

1.64 | ART 2 SEC 2 CL 2

ambassador a country's highest-ranking diplomatic representative in another country or at an international organization

public minister another diplomatic representative of one country in another

consul a person appointed by the government of a country to look after the interests of its businesses and travelers in a city of another country

judges of the Supreme Court justices of the Supreme Court

other officers judges of inferior courts, heads of departments, persons occupying other civilian positions that have significant authority (not simply government employees), and commissioned officers of the armed forces and the other uniformed services such as the Public Health Service

all other officers of the United States whose appointments are not herein otherwise provided for all other officers of the United States except the officers of the two houses of Congress (Clauses 1.6 and 1.12), many inferior officers (Clause 1.66), and officers of the National Guard when on active duty in the service of the United States (Clauses 2.22–2.24)

which shall be whose offices shall be

---

* This clause is placed in Chapter 1 in order to show the treaty-making procedure next to the procedures for making laws and joint resolutions—like them, treaties are a kind of law.

   But treaty making should also be borne in mind when reading in Chapter 2 about executive powers in the national government (Clauses 2.31 to 2.34).

Making Recess Appointments

The President shall have power to fill all vacancies that may happen during the recess of the Senate, by granting commissions which shall expire at the end of its next session.

1.65 | ART 2 SEC 2 CL 3

happen exist (as used here)

recess of the Senate the period during which Congress is adjourned after each year's session; also, periods during the year when the Senate is adjourned for at least ten (perhaps) days

granting commissions making appointments (as used here)

commission a document authorizing a person to exercise the powers of an office

Providing for the Appointment of Inferior Officers

The Congress may by law vest the appointment of such inferior officers as it thinks proper in the President alone, in the heads of departments, or in the courts of law.

1.66 | ART 2 SEC 2 CL 2

vest the appointment place the power of appointment

heads of departments the heads or secretaries of the departments and the heads of the other major agencies (as used here)

Appropriations, Accounts

No money shall be drawn from the treasury but in consequence of appropriations made by law, and a regular statement and account of the receipts and expenditures of all public money shall be published from time to time.*

1.67 | ART 1 SEC 9 CL 7

drawn withdrawn, paid out

but in consequence of except as approved by

appropriation approval of the expenditure of a stated amount of money for a stated purpose

The President

Commissioning Officers

The President shall commission all the officers of the United States.

1.68 | ART 2 SEC 3

Obtaining the Opinions of Department Heads

He may require the opinion in writing of the principal officer in each of the executive departments, upon any subject relating to the duties of their respective offices.

1.69 | ART 2 SEC 2 CL 1

---

* No statement and account of the expenditures of the national intelligence agencies is published.

The Courts, the Congress, and the President

Original Jurisdiction of the Supreme Court

In all cases affecting ambassadors, other public ministers, and consuls, and those in which a state shall be a party, the Supreme Court shall have original jurisdiction.

1.70 | ART 3 SEC 2 CL 2

ambassadors, other public ministers, and consuls diplomats representing other countries (as used here)

party a participant in a court case, a plaintiff or defendant (as used here)

jurisdiction the authority to exercise the judicial power (the power to hear and decide cases) (as used here)

original jurisdiction the authority to hear and decide a case from its very beginning, without the previous involvement of any other court

Appellate Jurisdiction of the Supreme Court

In all the other cases mentioned below,* the Supreme Court shall have appellate jurisdiction both as to law and fact, with such exceptions and under such regulations as the Congress shall make, but

1.71 | ART 3 SEC 2 CL 2

all the other cases mentioned below all the other cases to which the judicial power of the national government extends

appellate (ə pel′ it) **jurisdiction** the authority to hear and decide appeals from the decisions of other (lower) courts

Findings of Fact by Juries in Suits at Common Law

in suits at common law, no fact tried by a jury shall be otherwise reexamined in any court of the United States than according to the rules of the common law.

1.72 | 7TH AMEND

suits at common law non-criminal cases in which the procedures of the common law (in contrast to equity or admiralty procedures) are followed

tried found out or determined in a trial (as used here)

the rules of the common law rules saying that, when a jury considers the facts of a case and gives a verdict, a higher court to which the case is appealed may only consider questions of law—it may not revise the jury's findings of fact

Creating Lower Courts

The Congress shall have power to constitute tribunals inferior to the Supreme Court.

1.73 | ART 1 SEC 8 CL 9

constitute tribunals establish courts

---

* In Clauses 2.36, 2.37, 2.39, 2.41, 2.43 (in part), and 7.42

Removal from Office

Scope of the Removal Power

The President, Vice President, and all civil officers of the United States shall be removed from office on impeachment for and conviction of treason, bribery, or other high crimes and misdemeanors.

1.74 | ART 2 SEC 4

civil officers officers of the national government except officers of the armed forces and members of Congress (as used here)

impeachment for accusation of

other high crimes and misdemeanors other important crimes and misconduct in office

Impeachment by the House of Representatives

The House of Representatives shall have the sole power of impeachment.

1.75 | ART 1 SEC 2 CL 5

the House of Representatives shall have the sole power only the House of Representatives shall have the power

Trial by the Senate

The Senate shall have the sole power to try all impeachments. When sitting for that purpose, the senators shall be on oath or affirmation. When the President of the United States is tried, the chief justice shall preside, and

no person shall be convicted without the concurrence of two-thirds of the members present.

1.76 | ART 1 SEC 3 CL 6

on oath bound by a promise to perform a duty or speak the truth; the promise begins "I swear" and declares or implies a belief in God

on affirmation bound by a promise to perform a duty or speak the truth; the promise begins "I affirm" and lacks any expression of religious belief

chief justice the presiding member of the Supreme Court

Judgment

Judgment in cases of impeachment shall not extend further than to removal from office and disqualification to hold and enjoy any office of honor, trust, or profit under the United States, but

the party convicted shall nevertheless be liable and subject to indictment, trial, judgment, and punishment, according to law.

1.77 | ART 1 SEC 3 CL 7

judgment a decision, order, or sentence of a court by which a civil or criminal proceeding is brought to an end

any office of honor, trust, or profit any office or position

indictment (in dyt′mənt) an accusation that a person has committed a crime

Limitation on Accepting Presents and Titles from Foreign States

No person holding any office of profit or trust under the United States shall, without the consent of the Congress, accept any present, emolument, office, or title of any kind whatever from any king, prince, or foreign state.

1.78 | ART 1 SEC 9 CL 8

Chapter 2
Powers of the National Government

Legislative Powers

The Congress shall have power*

2.1 | ART 1 SEC 8

Finance

Raising Revenue

to lay and collect taxes, duties, imposts, and excises, to pay the debts and provide for the common defense and general welfare of the United States, but

2.2 | ART 1 SEC 8 CL 1

lay impose

duties taxes on imports, tariffs (as used here)

imposts taxes and duties

excises taxes on the production or sale of goods or services and (as used here) various other kinds of taxes

to pay the debts in order to pay the debts

---

* The Constitution gives to Congress "all legislative powers herein granted" (Clause 1.1).

   Grants of legislative power are made throughout the Constitution:

   More than a dozen of the first 79 clauses grant power to provide for the organization and operation of the national government (such as the powers to set the date of presidential elections and to establish courts);

   the next group of clauses (2.1–2.30) set forth the national government's (and Congress's) legislative powers over a broad array of subjects (taxation, commerce, the armed forces, and others); and

   the later clauses contain some additional grants of legislative power, including power to enforce rights protected by the Constitution.

Ban on (Prohibition of) Taxing Exports

no tax or duty shall be laid on articles exported from any state,

2.3 | ART 1 SEC 9 CL 5

Geographic Uniformity of Indirect Taxes

all duties, imposts, and excises shall be uniform throughout the United States, and

2.4 | ART 1 SEC 8 CL 1

uniform throughout the United States imposed at the same rate in all parts of the country

Apportionment of Direct Taxes

no capitation or other direct tax shall be laid, unless in proportion to the census or enumeration hereinbefore directed to be taken; however,

2.5 | ART 1 SEC 9 CL 4

capitation a tax of a certain amount on each person, a head tax

other direct tax a tax on land

in proportion to the census/ apportionment among the several states collection of taxes from the taxable sources in each state, in amounts proportional to the populations of the states

Power to Tax Incomes

the Congress shall have power to lay and collect taxes on incomes, from whatever source derived, without apportionment among the several states and without regard to any census or enumeration;

2.6 | 16TH AMEND

hereinbefore above, previously in this document (in Clause 1.3)

Borrowing

to borrow money on the credit of the United States; and the validity of the public debt of the United States, authorized by law, shall not be questioned;

2.7 | ART 1 SEC 8 CL 2 & 14TH AMEND SEC 4

the validity of the public debt the legal force and binding character of the government's promise to repay the debt

Coinage

to coin money and regulate the value thereof, and of foreign coin;

2.8 | ART 1 SEC 8 CL 5

to coin money to produce money

Punishment of Counterfeiting

to provide for the punishment of counterfeiting the securities and current coin of the United States;

2.9 | ART 1 SEC 8 CL 6

counterfeiting producing an imitation and passing it off as the real thing

securities bonds and other certificates promising to repay debt

current coin money that is in use

Commerce

Regulating Commerce

to regulate commerce with foreign nations, and among the several states, and with the Indian tribes, but

2.10 | ART 1 SEC 8 CL 3

Ban on Transportation of Intoxicating Liquors into Any State, Territory, or Possession in Violation of Its Laws

the transportation or importation into any state, territory, or possession of the United States for delivery or use therein of intoxicating liquors, in violation of the laws thereof, is hereby prohibited;*

2.11 | 21ST AMEND SEC 2

therein in it

intoxicating liquors alcoholic beverages

Bankruptcies

to establish uniform laws on the subject of bankruptcies throughout the United States;

2.12 | ART 1 SEC 8 CL 4

bankruptcies inability of persons or organizations to pay their debts

Weights and Measures

to fix the standard of weights and measures;

2.13 | ART 1 SEC 8 CL 5

fix determine or establish

the standard of weights and measures the standards of weights and measures

Post Offices and Post Roads

to establish post offices and post roads;

2.14 | ART 1 SEC 8 CL 7

Copyrights and Patents

to promote the progress of science and useful arts, by securing for limited times to authors and inventors the exclusive right to their respective writings and discoveries;

2.15 | ART 1 SEC 8 CL 8

science knowledge

securing giving and protecting

limited times any time from a few years to a century or more (as used here)

the exclusive right to copyrights and patents on

---

* The national government's power to regulate commerce among the states, given in Clause 2.10, places severe limits on the power of the state governments to pass laws affecting such commerce. Clause 2.11 creates a small exception to this rule, giving the states slightly greater power over interstate commerce in alcoholic beverages than in other things.

Powers of the Nation in a World of Nations

Naturalization

to establish a uniform rule of naturalization;

2.16 | ART 1 SEC 8 CL 4

naturalization the procedure by which foreigners become citizens of a country—members of the political community, possessing the rights and duties that come with membership

Offenses on the High Seas and Against the Law of Nations

to define and punish piracies and felonies committed on the high seas, and offenses against the law of nations;

2.17 | ART 1 SEC 8 CL 10

the law of nations international law

Armed Forces and War

Declaring War

to declare war;

2.18 | ART 1 SEC 8 CL 11

Armies

to raise and support armies, but

2.19 | ART 1 SEC 8 CL 12

Two-Year Limit on Appropriations for the Army

no appropriation of money to that use shall be for a longer term than two years;

2.20 | ART 1 SEC 8 CL 12

The Navy

to provide and maintain a navy;

2.21 | ART 1 SEC 8 CL 13

Calling Forth the Militia

to provide for calling forth the militia to execute the laws of the union, suppress insurrections, and repel invasions;*

2.22 | ART 1 SEC 8 CL 15

calling forth calling to active duty in the service of the United States

militia National Guard

suppress put down

insurrection a rebellion or uprising

Organizing, Arming, Disciplining, and Governing the Militia

to provide for organizing, arming, and disciplining the militia, and for governing such part of them as may be employed in the service of the United States,

2.23 | ART 1 SEC 8 CL 16

disciplining prescribing regulations and training for

Appointment of Officers and Training Reserved to the States

reserving to the states the appointment of the officers and the authority of training the militia according to the discipline prescribed by Congress;

2.24 | ART 1 SEC 8 CL 16

Regulations for the Armed Forces

to make rules for the government and regulation of the land and naval forces;

2.25 | ART 1 SEC 8 CL 14

land and naval forces armed forces

Rules Concerning Captures

to make rules concerning captures on land and water;

2.26 | ART 1 SEC 8 CL 11

captures the capture of ships or other property by the armed forces

---

* In the early years of the Republic, the militia of each state was composed of men of military age, who were required to keep a firearm in readiness and could be called forth for military service.

    Today's locally based military force is provided by the state National Guards, and the Constitution's militia clauses (2.22–2.24) may generally be applied to them. But the Guard is very different from the old state militias. The personnel are armed, equipped, and paid by the national government, which has made them an integral part of the nation's armed forces (exercising the power to raise and support armies, given in Clause 2.19); it can use them not only to repel invasions but to fight in other countries.

Territory and Property of the National Government

The Seat of Government

to exercise exclusive legislation in all cases whatsoever, over such district (not exceeding ten miles square*) as may be the seat of the government of the United States;

2.27 | ART 1 SEC 8 CL 17

Field Establishments

to exercise like authority over all places purchased by the consent of the legislature of the state in which the same shall be, for the erection of forts, magazines, arsenals, dockyards, and other needful buildings;

2.28 | ART 1 SEC 8 CL 17

magazine a place for storing weapons, and especially explosives

arsenal a place for manufacturing or storing weapons and military equipment

dockyard a place for building and repairing warships

Territory and Other Property

to dispose of and make all needful rules and regulations respecting the territory or other property belonging to the United States; and

2.29 | ART 4 SEC 3 CL 2

Laws Necessary and Proper

to make all laws which shall be necessary and proper for carrying into execution the foregoing powers, and all other powers vested by this Constitution in the government of the United States or in any department or officer thereof.

2.30 | ART 1 SEC 8 CL 18

necessary and proper appropriate, suited to the purpose

* The District of Columbia at first occupied a ten-mile square of territory provided by Maryland and Virginia. In 1846 Virginia's contribution was returned to it, reducing the District's area to 68.3 square miles (177.0 square kilometers).

Executive Powers

Faithful Execution of the Laws

The President* shall take care that the laws be faithfully executed;

2.31 | ART 2 SEC 3

Receiving Ambassadors

shall receive ambassadors and other public ministers;

2.32 | ART 2 SEC 3

Commander in Chief of the Armed Forces

shall be commander in chief of the army and navy of the United States, and of the militia of the several states when called into the actual service of the United States; and

commander in chief highest commander, over all

army and navy armed forces (as used here)

2.33 | ART 2 SEC 2 CL 1

Granting Reprieves and Pardons

shall have power to grant reprieves and pardons for offenses against the United States, except in cases of impeachment.

reprieve an order delaying a punishment

pardon an order freeing a person from punishment for a crime

2.34 | ART 2 SEC 2 CL 1

---

* The Constitution grants the executive power in Clause 1.19: "The executive power shall be vested in a President of the United States." It also gives the President power to negotiate treaties (Clause 1.63) and requires the President to take an oath to "faithfully execute the office of President" (Clause 6.4).

The President is also, in Clauses 1.57–1.69 and 1.73, given some powers in the organization and operation of the national government, such as making appointments and participation in making the laws.

Scope of the Judicial Power

The judicial power shall extend*

2.35 | ART 3 SEC 2 CL 1

Kinds of Laws or Persons

The Constitution, Laws, and Treaties of the United States

to all cases in law and equity arising under this Constitution, the laws of the United States, and treaties made under the authority of the United States;

2.36 | ART 3 SEC 2 CL 1

law and equity common law and equity, the two main kinds of legal jurisdiction and procedure. There were formerly separate courts for each, but the two are now merged, so a single lawsuit can make use of both procedures.

Admiralty and Maritime Jurisdiction

to all cases of admiralty and maritime jurisdiction;

2.37 | ART 3 SEC 2 CL 1

admiralty and maritime jurisdiction another kind of legal jurisdiction, covering shipping and happenings on the oceans and on inland waters that ships are able to use

Foreign Diplomats

to all cases affecting ambassadors, other public ministers, and consuls;

2.38 | ART 3 SEC 2 CL 1

Kinds of Parties

The United States

to controversies to which the United States shall be a party;

2.39 | ART 3 SEC 2 CL 1

controversy dispute, disagreement

Two or More States

to controversies between two or more states,

2.40 | ART 3 SEC 2 CL 1

---

* The Constitution grants the judicial power in Clause 1.48: "The judicial power of the United States shall be vested in one Supreme Court, and in such inferior courts as the Congress may from time to time ordain and establish."

Citizens of Different States

between citizens of different states,

2.41 | ART 3 SEC 2 CL 1

States, Citizens, and Foreign States and Persons
A State and Citizens of Another State

between a state and citizens of another state, and

2.42 | ART 3 SEC 2 CL 1

A State or Its Citizens and Foreign States or Persons

between a state, or the citizens thereof, and foreign states, citizens, or subjects; but

2.43 | ART 3 SEC 2 CL 1

Ban on Exercise of the Judicial Power in Suits of Persons Against States

the judicial power of the United States shall not be construed to extend to any suit in law or equity, commenced or prosecuted against one of the states by citizens of another state, or by citizens or subjects of any foreign state.*

construed interpreted

2.44 | 11TH AMEND

---

* The Supreme Court has also banned such suits in admiralty and maritime cases; also prohibited are suits against a state by its own citizens and by Indian tribes.

Chapter 3
The States

The National Government and the States

Admitting New States

New states may be admitted by the Congress into this union, but

no new state shall be formed or erected within the jurisdiction of any other state, nor any state be formed by the junction of two or more states or parts of states, without the consent of the legislatures of the states concerned as well as of the Congress.

3.1 | ART 4 SEC 3 CL 1

jurisdiction of any state the area in which a state exercises the power to govern (as used here)

junction a joining or combining

Guarantee of a Republican Form of Government

The United States shall guarantee to every state in this union a republican form of government, and

3.2 | ART 4 SEC 4

republican form of government government by persons elected by the people—no king, queen, or (as used here) nobles—with liberty and justice

Protection Against Invasion and Domestic Violence

shall protect each of them against invasion, and on application of the legislature or of the executive (when the legislature cannot be convened), against domestic violence.

domestic violence disturbance or rebellion within the country, lack of peace and calm

3.3 | ART 4 SEC 4

Ban on Preference to the Ports of Any State

No preference shall be given by any regulation of commerce or revenue to the ports of one state over those of another, nor shall vessels bound to or from one state be obliged to enter, clear, or pay duties in another.

vessel ship

enter upon sailing into the waters of a country, report to a customs office (where the national government collects duties and enforces its regulations of commerce) and comply with its requirements

clear before leaving the waters of a country, report to a customs office and comply with its requirements

3.4 | ART 1 SEC 9 CL 6

Limitations on the States

Finance

Money

No state shall coin money, emit bills of credit, or make anything but gold and silver coin a tender in payment of debts.

emit bills of credit issue paper money

tender something that the law requires everyone to accept as money

3.5 | ART 1 SEC 10 CL 1

Duties of Tonnage

No state shall, without the consent of Congress, lay any duty of tonnage.

duty of tonnage a charge imposed on a ship for the privilege of using a port, the amount being usually based on the ship's cargo-carrying capacity

3.6 | ART 1 SEC 10 CL 3

Duties on Imports and Exports

No state shall, without the consent of the Congress, lay any imposts or duties on imports or exports except what may be absolutely necessary for executing its inspection laws, and

the net produce of all duties and imposts laid by any state on imports or exports shall be for the use of the treasury of the United States, and all such laws shall be subject to the revision and control of the Congress.

3.7 | ART 1 SEC 10 CL 2

net produce (proh′dooss) net revenues (revenues in excess of inspection costs, as used here)

for the use of paid into

Foreign Relations

Treaties, Alliances, and Confederations

No state shall enter into any treaty, alliance, or confederation,

3.8 | ART 1 SEC 10 CL 1

confederation a league or association of states having a stronger and more permanent organization than an alliance

Agreements and Compacts

nor shall any state, without the consent of Congress, enter into any agreement or compact with a foreign power.

3.9 | ART 1 SEC 10 CL 3

compact formal agreement

Armed Forces and War

Troops and Ships of War

No state shall, without the consent of Congress, keep troops or ships of war in time of peace,

3.10 | ART 1 SEC 10 CL 3

troops . . . in time of peace a standing army

Engaging in War

or engage in war, unless actually invaded or in such imminent danger as will not admit of delay.

3.11 | ART 1 SEC 10 CL 3

imminent danger a likelihood that something harmful will happen very soon

admit of allow, permit

Relations Among the States

Full Faith and Credit to the Public Acts, Records, and Judicial Proceedings of Other States

Full faith and credit shall be given in each state to the public acts, records, and judicial proceedings of every other state, and

the Congress may by general laws prescribe the manner in which such acts, records, and proceedings shall be proved, and the effect thereof.

3.12 | ART 4 SEC 1

full faith and credit full recognition and enforcement

public acts, records, and judicial proceedings of every other state the laws (other than criminal laws) of another state, the documents produced or recorded in its courts, and the judgments and orders of its courts

Interstate Compacts

No state shall, without the consent of Congress, enter into any agreement or compact with another state.*

3.13 | ART 1 SEC 10 CL 3

agreement or compact with another state an agreement or compact between states that increases the political power of any state in relation to the national government

Returning Fugitives from Justice

A person charged in any state with treason, felony, or other crime who shall flee from justice and be found in another state shall, on demand of the executive authority of the state from which he fled, be delivered up, to be removed to the state having jurisdiction of the crime.

3.14 | ART 4 SEC 2 CL 2

Powers Reserved to the States or to the People

The powers not delegated to the United States by the Constitution, nor prohibited by it to the states, are reserved to the states respectively, or to the people.

3.15 | 10TH AMEND

delegated assigned, entrusted

---

* While this clause is worded as a limitation, the national government has encouraged the states to use compacts to deal with their common problems, and has approved many interstate compacts.

Chapter 4
Citizenship and the Right to Vote

Citizenship in Nation and State

All persons born or naturalized in the United States and subject to the jurisdiction thereof are citizens of the United States and of the state wherein they reside.

The Congress shall have power to enforce this clause by appropriate legislation.

4.1 | 14TH AMEND SECS 1 & 5

subject to the jurisdiction thereof excluding children born to foreign diplomats stationed in the United States and to alien members of enemy armed forces

Removal of Restrictions on the Right to Vote

Race or Color

The right of citizens of the United States to vote shall not be denied or abridged by the United States or by any state on account of race or color.

4.2 | 15TH AMEND SEC 1

abridged reduced, taken away

Sex

The right of citizens of the United States to vote shall not be denied or abridged by the United States or by any state on account of sex.

4.3 | 19TH AMEND

Age (Eighteen Years or Older)

The right of citizens of the United States who are eighteen years of age or older to vote shall not be denied or abridged by the United States or by any state on account of age.

4.4 | 26TH AMEND SEC 1

Poll Tax or Other Tax

The right of citizens of the United States to vote in any primary or other election shall not be denied or abridged by the United States or any state by reason of failure to pay any poll tax or other tax.

4.5 | 24TH AMEND SEC 1

primary election an election in which voters choose candidates to run for office in the final (general) election

poll (pohl) **tax** a tax that a person must pay in order to vote

Power to Enforce the Right to Vote

The Congress shall have power to enforce the right of citizens to vote by appropriate legislation.

4.6 | 15TH, 19TH, 24TH, & 26TH AMENDS, SEC 2 OF EACH

the right of citizens to vote the right protected by Clauses 4.2–4.5 and 7.13

Chapter 5
Rights and Equality

Limitations on Both the National Government and the States

Due Process of Law

No person shall be deprived of life, liberty, or property without due process of law.

The Congress shall have power to enforce this clause by appropriate legislation.

5.1 | 5TH AMEND & 14TH AMEND SECS 1 & 5

person a person, whether a citizen or not; also, a corporation (as used here)

deprive a person of liberty take away a person's liberty

due process of law fair procedure, good reason for a governmental action that deprives, and preservation of fundamental freedoms; justice

Equal Protection of the Laws

No state* shall deny to any person within its jurisdiction the equal protection of the laws.

The Congress shall have power to enforce this clause by appropriate legislation.

5.2 | 14TH AMEND SECS 1 & 5

equal protection of the laws treatment in the same manner as other persons in similar situations, free from unjustified discrimination on the basis of race, sex, or other personal or social characteristics

* This clause, a part of the 14th Amendment, originally applied only to the states, but it now also applies to the national government in much the same way. The Supreme Court has ruled that the due process clause (5.1) prohibits the national government from denying equal protection of the laws to persons within its jurisdiction.

Ban on Slavery and Involuntary Servitude

Neither slavery nor involuntary servitude, except as a punishment for crime whereof the party shall have been duly convicted, shall exist within the United States or any place subject to its jurisdiction.

The Congress shall have power to enforce this clause by appropriate legislation.

5.3 | 13TH AMEND SECS 1 & 2

involuntary servitude unwilling, forced labor

Ban on Titles of Nobility

No title of nobility shall be granted by the United States or by any state.

5.4 | ART 1 SEC 9 CL 8 & ART 1 SEC 10 CL 1

title of nobility a position or rank in an aristocracy, such as duchess or count

Ban on Religious Tests for Public Office

No religious test shall ever be required as a qualification for any office or public trust under the United States.*

5.5 | ART 6 CL 3

religious test a declaration that one holds a certain religious belief

public trust a responsibility or duty in the operation of the government

First-Amendment Freedoms

No Law Respecting an Establishment of Religion, Free Exercise of Religion

Congress† shall make no law respecting an establishment of religion or prohibiting the free exercise thereof, or

5.6 | 1ST AMEND

Freedom of Speech and the Press

abridging the freedom of speech or of the press or

5.7 | 1ST AMEND

---

* The ban on religious tests, a part of the original Constitution that at first applied only to the national government, now also applies to the states. The Supreme Court has declared that such tests infringe on the religious freedom protected by Clause 5.6.

† Clauses 5.6–5.12 and 5.14–5.17 are parts of the Bill of Rights, which originally applied only to the national government, but these clauses now also apply to the states. The Supreme Court has ruled that the due process clause (5.1) prohibits the states from infringing rights, such as these, that are fundamental in our system of liberty and justice.

Right to Assemble and Petition

the right of the people peaceably to assemble and to petition the government for a redress of grievances.

5.8 | 1ST AMEND

redress (ree'dress) **of grievances** the setting right of wrongs that are complained of

Just Compensation for Private Property Taken

Private property shall not be taken for public use without just compensation.

5.9 | 5TH AMEND

public use public use or public purpose

Right to Keep and Bear Arms

A well regulated militia being necessary to the security of a free state,* the right of the people to keep and bear arms shall not be infringed.

5.10 | 2ND AMEND

state a people and their government (as used here)

infringed violated

Rights in Governmental Investigations and Arrests

Freedom from Unreasonable Searches and Seizures

The right of the people to be secure in their persons, houses, papers, and effects against unreasonable searches and seizures shall not be violated, and

effects belongings, personal property

no warrants shall issue but upon probable cause, supported by oath or affirmation, and particularly describing the place to be searched and the persons or things to be seized.

5.11 | 4TH AMEND

warrant a document produced by an officer of the government, giving an order; here, an order by a judge or other officer of a court, authorizing a search, seizure, or arrest

issue come forth, be produced

probable cause reason to believe that a crime has been or is being committed, and that a particular search or seizure is justified

---

* This opening statement of purpose does not limit the right to keep and bear arms to members of state militias, or to their modern successors in the National Guard.

Ban on Compelling Testimony Against Oneself

No person shall be compelled in any criminal case to be a witness against himself.*

5.12 | 5TH AMEND

Prohibition of Some Unjust Prosecutions

Ban on Bills of Attainder and Ex Post Facto Laws

No bill of attainder or ex post facto law shall be passed.

5.13 | ART 1 SEC 9 CL 3 & ART 1 SEC 10 CL 1

bill of attainder a bill that, when it is passed, convicts and punishes a person or persons named or identified by it, not allowing them a trial in a court

ex post facto (Latin: "after the deed") **law** a law that punishes an action performed before the law was passed, or increases the punishment for such an action, or reduces or changes the evidence needed to find someone guilty of it

Ban on Double Jeopardy

No person shall be subject for the same offense to be twice put in jeopardy of life or limb.

5.14 | 5TH AMEND

subject liable, required

put in jeopardy (jep′ər dee) **of life or limb** put in danger of conviction and punishment, prosecuted

Rights in Criminal Prosecutions

Right to Trial by Jury and Assistance of Counsel

In all criminal prosecutions,† the accused shall enjoy the right to a speedy and public trial by an impartial jury,‡ to have the assistance of counsel for his defense,

5.15 | 6TH AMEND

impartial not biased or prejudiced

jury a group of persons appointed by a court to sit through a trial and to give a verdict (a finding or decision) in the case

counsel a lawyer

Right to Be Informed of the Accusation

to be informed of the nature and cause of the accusation,

5.16 | 6TH AMEND

---

* This right exists not only in investigations (criminal or not) and arrests, but in trials and all other parts of a criminal case.

† Another right of the accused is the ban on compelling testimony against oneself (Clause 5.12).

‡ This clause does not give a right to a jury trial in prosecutions for lesser offenses (those punishable by no more than six months confinement) or in courts for juveniles (young people).

Rights with Respect to Witnesses

to be confronted with the witnesses against him, and
to have compulsory process for obtaining witnesses in
his favor.

5.17 | 6TH AMEND

compulsory process court orders
requiring persons to appear in court

Limitation on Bail

Excessive bail shall not be required,*

5.18 | 8TH AMEND

bail money or property deposited with
a court as assurance that an accused
person, set free until the trial, will return

Limitations on Punishment

nor excessive fines imposed,† nor cruel and unusual punishments inflicted.

5.19 | 8TH AMEND

Rights Retained by the People

The enumeration in the Constitution of certain rights
shall not be construed to deny or disparage others
retained by the people.‡

5.20 | 9TH AMEND

enumeration listing (as used here)

disparage belittle, lessen

---

* The Supreme Court has never declared that the ban on excessive
  bail applies to the states, but many lower courts of the United
  States have done so. It seems likely that the Supreme Court
  would rule a state-imposed bail (for a person who is entitled to
  bail) unconstitutional if the Court deemed it excessive.

† The Supreme Court has never applied the ban on excessive fines
  to the states, but it seems likely that a state-imposed fine would
  be struck down if the Court deemed it excessive.

‡ The Supreme Court has never declared that this part of the Bill
  of Rights applies to the states, though opinions of the Court and
  other courts have mentioned this, along with other parts of the
  Constitution, in support of a few decisions that dealt with state
  powers. If the clause ever serves as a basis for any of the Court's
  decisions, it seems as likely to be applied to the states as to the
  national government.

Limitations on the National Government

Right to Trial by Jury in Suits at Common Law

In suits at common law, the right of trial by jury shall be preserved.

5.21 | 7TH AMEND

suits at common law non-criminal cases that involve rights and remedies of a kind that were being enforced by the procedures of the common law (in contrast to equity or admiralty procedures) in 1791, when this clause was adopted (as used here)

Limitation on Quartering Soldiers in Houses

No soldier shall in time of peace be quartered in any house without the consent of the owner, nor in time of war but in a manner to be prescribed by law.*

5.22 | 3RD AMEND

quartered assigned to be housed and fed

Limitation on Suspending the Writ of Habeas Corpus

The privilege of the writ of habeas corpus shall not be suspended, unless when in cases of rebellion or invasion the public safety may require it.

5.23 | ART 1 SEC 9 CL 2

writ of habeas corpus (hay′bee ass kor′ pass) (Latin: "you shall have the body") a court order requiring that a person who is being held in custody be brought before a judge, and that the reason for holding the person be stated. If a lawful reason is not shown, the judge orders the person released. The writ may also be used to secure a review by a United States court of the process (arrest, trial, sentencing) by which a person has been sent to prison.

unless except

---

* A United States appeals court has declared that this clause applies to the states. The Supreme Court has never ruled on this issue.

Rights in Criminal Prosecutions

Indictment by Grand Jury

No person shall be held to answer for a capital or otherwise infamous crime, unless on an indictment of a grand jury, except in cases arising in the land or naval forces, or in the militia when in actual service in time of war or public danger.

5.24 | 5TH AMEND

held to answer prosecuted, put on trial

capital crime a crime punishable by death

infamous (in′fə məss) **crime** a crime punishable by more than a short prison term

indictment an accusation that a person has committed a crime, made by a grand jury, based on an accusation and evidence submitted to it by a prosecuting attorney

grand jury a group of persons appointed by a court to consider information about crimes that are said to have been committed, and to decide whether there is sufficient evidence to justify accusing any persons and bringing them to trial

Location of Trial, Jury of the State and District

The trial of all crimes, except in cases of impeachment, shall be by jury, shall be held in the state where the said crimes shall have been committed, and shall be by a jury of the state and district wherein the crimes shall have been committed, which district shall have been previously ascertained by law, but

when not committed within any state, the trial shall be at such place or places as the Congress may by law have directed.

5.25 | ART 3 SEC 2 CL 3 & 6TH AMEND

The Crime of Treason: Definition, Proof, and Punishment

Treason against the United States shall consist only in levying war against it or in adhering to its enemies, giving them aid and comfort. No person shall be convicted of treason unless on the testimony of two witnesses to the same overt act, or on confession in open court.

The Congress shall have power to declare the punishment of treason.

5.26 | ART 3 SEC 3 CLS 1 & 2

levying starting, waging

adhering to attaching oneself to, supporting

overt (oh′vərt) open to view, not hidden

Limitations on the States

The Obligation of Contracts

No state shall pass any law impairing the obligation of contracts.

5.27 | ART 1 SEC 10 CL 1

impairing diminishing, weakening

the obligation of contracts the requirement that contracts be fulfilled and obeyed

Privileges and/or Immunities of Citizens

Citizens of Each State

The citizens of each state shall be entitled to all privileges and immunities of citizens in the several states.

5.28 | ART 4 SEC 2 CL 1

citizen resident (as used here)

immunity an exemption from some legal requirements, granted to some persons

privileges and immunities a small number of rights, including the right to travel into a state and to live and work there

the several states any other state in which these persons happen to be, or in which they wish to visit or do business

Citizens of the United States

No state shall make or enforce any law which shall abridge the privileges or immunities of citizens of the United States.

The Congress shall have power to enforce this clause by appropriate legislation.

5.29 | 14TH AMEND SECS 1 & 5

privileges or immunities of citizens of the United States rights given by the Constitution, laws, and treaties of the United States

Chapter 6
The Constitution

Amending the Constitution
Proposing Amendments

The Congress, whenever two-thirds of both houses shall deem it necessary, shall propose amendments to this Constitution, or on the application of the legislatures of two-thirds of the several states, shall call a convention for proposing amendments,

6.1 | ART 5

deem think, believe

on the application at the request

convention an assembly of persons elected or appointed to take some governmental or political action

amendment addition, removal, or change

Ratifying Amendments

which in either case shall be valid to all intents and purposes as part of this Constitution, when ratified by the legislatures of three-fourths of the several states or by conventions in three-fourths thereof, as the one or the other mode of ratification may be proposed by the Congress.

6.2 | ART 5

to all intents and purposes for all practical purposes, completely

ratified approved

mode method

Limitation on Depriving Any State of Its Equal Representation in the Senate

But no state, without its consent, shall be deprived of its equal suffrage in the Senate.

suffrage right to vote, voting power

6.3 | ART 5

Oaths of Office, Supporting and Defending the Constitution

The President

Before the President enters on the execution of his office, he shall take the following oath or affirmation:*

enters on the execution of begins to serve in

"I do solemnly swear (or affirm) that I will faithfully execute the office of President of the United States, and will to the best of my ability preserve, protect, and defend the Constitution of the United States."

6.4 | ART 2 SEC 1 CL 8

Other Officials

The senators and representatives before mentioned, and the members of the several state legislatures, and all executive and judicial officers, both of the United States and of the several states, shall be bound by oath or affirmation to support this Constitution.

6.5 | ART 6 CL 3

---

* The name of the President-elect is inserted at the beginning: "I, George Washington, do solemnly . . . "

If the word "swear" is used, this becomes an oath, not an affirmation, and it customarily ends with an additional phrase: ". . . defend the Constitution of the United States, so help me God."

The Supreme Law of the Land

This Constitution, and the laws of the United States which shall be made in pursuance thereof, and all treaties made under the authority of the United States shall be the supreme law of the land, and the judges in every state shall be bound thereby, anything in the constitution or laws of any state to the contrary notwithstanding.

6.6 | ART 6 CL 2

in pursuance thereof in exercising the powers granted by it, in accordance with it

anything . . . notwithstanding despite anything . . .

HOW TO READ THE CONSTITUTION OF THE PAST

This chapter contains those parts of the Constitution that no longer have any effect.

The manner in which each clause has moved to The Constitution of the Past is indicated by a circled capital letter:

(P)   Served its purpose

(R)   Repealed (removed from the Constitution) by an amendment

(W)   Words repeated with changes by an amendment—repealed implicitly (without saying so)

(S)   Subject matter abolished by an amendment—repealed implicitly

(O)   Obsolete: the subject matter or situation has disappeared and is not likely to return

(C)   A Supreme Court decision or rule has established a broader right or protection, not limited in the manner stated by the words of the Constitution

These notations show that more than one-third of the clauses in The Constitution of the Past have served their purposes, more than one-third have been repealed, explicitly or implicitly, and most of the rest have been made obsolete by changes in American society and in the world.

While the headings are not written in the past tense, they describe the document as it existed in the past; they do not describe today's Constitution.

Footnotes explain why the provisions that are marked obsolete belong here.

Some parts of The Constitution of the Past are not full sentences. To show these in understandable form, each is accompanied by language with which it originally appeared, which is still in force and is here placed in brackets.

Thus in Clause 7.3, the first words set the stage for an action that was to be taken in 1789. Those words are now obsolete:

Immediately after they shall be assembled in consequence of the first election,

The bracketed phrase below, copied from Clause 1.8, is still in force. It tells who "they" are (the senators) and what is to be done to them (divided):

[the senators shall be divided as equally as may be into three classes].

To repeat: the text in large brackets is still in force and is part of today's Constitution.

Chapter 7
The Constitution of the Past

Starting the Government Under the Constitution

The First Census

[The actual enumeration shall be made]

within three years after the first meeting of the Congress of the United States, and

[within every] subsequent [term of ten years].

7.1 | ART 1 SEC 2 CL 3 | Ⓟ

Initial Apportionment of the House of Representatives

And until such enumeration shall be made,
the state of New Hampshire shall be entitled
to choose   3 representatives
     Massachusetts   8
     Rhode Island and   1
     Providence Plantations
     Connecticut   5
     New York   6

Ⓟ Served its purpose

55

New Jersey	4
Pennsylvania	8
Delaware	1
Maryland	6
Virginia	10
North Carolina	5
South Carolina	5
Georgia	3

7.2 | ART 1 SEC 2 CL 3 | Ⓟ

Giving Overlapping Terms to the First Senators

Immediately after they shall be assembled in consequence of the first election,

[the senators shall be divided as equally as may be into three classes].

The seats of the senators of the first class shall be vacated at the expiration of the second year, of the second class at the expiration of the fourth year, and of the third class at the expiration of the sixth year

[, so that one-third may be chosen every second year].

7.3 | ART 1 SEC 3 CL 2 | Ⓟ

Citizens at the Time of the Adoption of the Constitution Are Eligible to Be President

[No person except a natural born citizen],

or a citizen [of the United States] at the time of the adoption of this Constitution,

[shall be eligible to the office of President].

7.4 | ART 2 SEC 1 CL 5 | Ⓟ

Ⓟ Served its purpose

Acquiring Territory
for the Seat of Government

[The Congress shall have power . . . to exercise exclusive legislation in all cases whatsoever, over such district (not exceeding ten miles square) as may],

by cession of particular states and the acceptance of Congress,

cession (of) a transfer or surrender of governmental power (jurisdiction) over some territory (by)

[be]come [the seat of the government of the United States].

7.5 | ART 1 SEC 8 CL 17 | Ⓟ

Recognition of the Previous
Commitments of the United States

Continuing Validity of the Debts and Agreements of the Confederation

All debts contracted and engagements entered into before the adoption of this Constitution shall be as valid against the United States under this Constitution as under the Confederation.

engagement agreement, promise

Confederation the government of the United States before the adoption of the Constitution

7.6 | ART 6 CL 1 | Ⓟ

Separate Mention of Treaties Made Before Adoption of the Constitution and Those Made Thereafter
Covered by the Judicial Power

[The judicial power shall extend to all cases in law and equity arising under this Constitution, the laws of the United States, and treaties made],

or which shall be made,*

[under its authority].

7.7 | ART 3 SEC 2 CL 1 | Ⓟ

---

* A few treaties, or parts of treaties, that were made before adoption of the Constitution (almost all of them with Native American tribes) still have force. But there is no longer a need for separate mention of these ("treaties made") and all treaties made after 1788 ("which shall be made"). A single "treaties made" covers all past and future treaties.

Ⓟ Served its purpose

Included in the Supreme Law of the Land

[This Constitution, and the laws of the United States which shall be made in pursuance thereof, and all treaties made],

or which shall be made,

[under the authority of the United States shall be the supreme law of the land].

7.8 | ART 6 CL 2 | Ⓟ

Slavery and the Slaves

Establishment of Slavery in the Constitution

Inclusion of Three-fifths of the Slaves in the Population on Which Apportionment of Representatives and Direct Taxes Is Based

[Representatives and direct taxes shall be apportioned among the several states which may be included within this union according to their respective numbers, which shall be determined by adding to the whole number of]

free

[persons, including those bound to service for a term of years and excluding Indians not taxed,]*

three-fifths of all other persons.

7.9 | ART 1 SEC 2 CL 3 | Ⓢ

those bound to service for a term of years indentured servants, who were required to work for their masters for a certain time

Indians not taxed the Native Americans, except any who were so well integrated into the white people's society that they were subject to taxation

all other persons the slaves

Ⓟ Served its purpose

Ⓢ Subject matter abolished by an amendment (implicitly repealed)

* In this clause, the language shown in brackets is obsolete like the non-bracketed language, as is shown in Clause 7.18.

Requirement That Slaves Escaping into Another State Be Returned to Their Owners

No person held to service or labor in one state under the laws thereof, escaping into another, shall in consequence of any law or regulation therein be discharged from such service or labor, but shall be delivered up on claim of the party to whom such service or labor may be due.

7.10 | ART 4 SEC 2 CL 3 | Ⓢ

person held to service or labor a slave or an indentured servant

party person (as used here)

Temporary Ban on Laws Prohibiting the Slave Trade

The migration or importation of such persons as any of the states now existing shall think proper to admit shall not be prohibited by the Congress prior to the year 1808, but a tax or duty may be imposed on such importation, not exceeding ten dollars for each person.

7.11 | ART 1 SEC 9 CL 1 | Ⓟ Ⓢ

such persons as any of the states now existing shall think proper to admit slaves

Temporary Ban on Constitutional Amendments Affecting the Slave Trade and the Requirement That Direct Taxes Be Apportioned

No amendment to the Constitution which may be made prior to the year 1808 shall in any manner affect the first and fourth clauses in the ninth section of the first article.

7.12 | ART 5 | Ⓟ

the first and fourth clauses in the ninth section of the first article Clause 7.11 (temporary ban on prohibition of the slave trade) and Clause 2.5 (requirement that direct taxes be apportioned)

The Right of Former Slaves to Vote

[The right of citizens of the United States to vote shall not be denied or abridged by the United States or by any state on account of race or color]

or previous condition of servitude.

7.13 | 15TH AMEND SEC 1 | Ⓟ Ⓢ

servitude enslavement (as used here)

Ⓟ Served its purpose

Ⓢ Subject matter abolished by an amendment (implicitly repealed)

The Civil War

Civil War Debts and Claims

Validity of the Debts Incurred by the United States in Fighting the Civil War

[The validity of the public debt of the United States, authorized by law,]

including debts incurred for payment of pensions and bounties for services in suppressing insurrection or rebellion,

bounty reward, grant

[shall not be questioned].*

7.14 | 14TH AMEND SEC 4 | Ⓟ

Ban on Paying the Debts of the Confederacy and Compensating Slave Owners

But neither the United States nor any state shall assume or pay any debt or obligation incurred in aid of insurrection or rebellion against the United States, or any claim for the loss or emancipation of any slave, but all such debts, obligations, and claims shall be held illegal and void.

emancipation setting free, liberation

7.15 | 14TH AMEND SEC 4 | Ⓟ

Limitation on Officeholding by Some Former Confederates

No person shall be a senator or representative in Congress or elector of President and Vice President, or hold any office, civil or military, under the United States or under any state,

who, having previously taken an oath as a member of Congress, or as an officer of the United States, or as a member of any state legislature, or as an executive or judicial officer of any state, to support the Constitution of the United States,

---

* The power of Congress to enforce the 14th Amendment by legislation, stated in Clauses 4.1, 5.1, 5.2, and 5.29, also applies to Clauses 1.3, 2.7, 7.14–7.16, 7.19, and 7.20.

Ⓟ Served its purpose

shall have engaged in insurrection or rebellion against the same, or given aid or comfort to the enemies thereof.

But Congress may, by a vote of two-thirds of each house, remove such disability.

7.16 | 14TH AMEND SEC 3 | Ⓟ

disability limitation, disqualification (as used here)

The Congress

Representation in the House

Minimum Number of Persons per Representative

The number of representatives shall not exceed one for every thirty thousand.*

7.17 | ART 1 SEC 2 CL 3 | ◎

the number of representatives shall not exceed one for every thirty thousand the number of persons per representative shall not be less than 30,000

Determination of the Population on Which Apportionment Is Based
Apportionment of Representatives and Direct Taxes; Inclusion of Indentured Servants and Exclusion of Indians Not Taxed

Representatives and direct taxes† shall be apportioned among the several states which may be included within this union according to their respective numbers, which shall be determined by adding to the whole number of

[free]

persons, including those bound to service for a term of years and excluding Indians not taxed,‡

[three-fifths of all other persons].

7.18 | ART 1 SEC 2 CL 3 | Ⓦ ◎

---

* This limitation was soon deprived of all effect by the rapid growth of the country's population. The approximate number of persons per representative increased from 35,000 after the census of 1800 to 193,000 after 1900 and 647,000 after 2000.

† This statement of the requirement that direct taxes be apportioned was not included when this sentence was repeated, with changes, in the 14th Amendment (see Clause 7.19), so it has been implicitly repealed. But the requirement remains a part of today's Constitution, being also stated in Clause 2.5.

‡ All Native Americans are now subject to taxation by the national government.

Ⓟ Served its purpose

Ⓦ Words repeated with changes by an amendment (implicitly repealed)

◎ Obsolete: the subject matter or situation has disappeared and is not likely to return

*Counting the Whole Number of Persons;
Another Exclusion of Indians Not Taxed*

[Representatives shall be apportioned among the several states according to their respective numbers,]

counting the whole number of persons in each state, excluding Indians not taxed.

7.19 | 14TH AMEND SEC 2 | Ⓟ ◎

counting the whole number of persons that is, not counting some people as equal to only three-fifths of a person—affirming, for the nation that had just emerged from the Civil War, the implicit repeal of the three-fifths rule of apportionment that resulted from the abolition of slavery

Reduction in Representation of States in Which the Right of Some Male Inhabitants to Vote Is Denied or Abridged

But when the right to vote at any election for the choice of electors for President and Vice President of the United States, representatives in Congress, the executive and judicial officers of a state, or the members of the legislature thereof

is denied to any of the male inhabitants of such state, being twenty-one years of age and citizens of the United States, or in any way abridged except for participation in rebellion or other crime,

the basis of representation therein shall be reduced in the proportion which the number of such male citizens shall bear to the whole number of male citizens twenty-one years of age in such state.*

7.20 | 14TH AMEND SEC 2 | ◎

the basis of representation therein the population used to calculate the state's number of seats in the House of Representatives

---

* This clause was intended to give the national government a means of encouraging states to allow black men to vote. It might have been used for this purpose, even after the Constitution was amended to prohibit denial of the right to vote on account of race or color (Clause 4.2), since many states prevented their black populations from voting despite the amendment. But it was never so used. It became obsolete when black people truly gained the right to vote in every state.

Ⓟ Served its purpose

◎ Obsolete: the subject matter or situation has disappeared and is not likely to return

Choosing Senators

Election of Senators by State Legislatures

The Senate of the United States shall be composed of two senators from each state, chosen by the legislature thereof for six years, and each senator shall have one vote.

7.21 | ART 1 SEC 3 CL 1 | Ⓦ

Filling Vacancies

If vacancies happen by resignation or otherwise, during the recess of the legislature of any state, the executive thereof may make temporary appointments until the next meeting of the legislature, which shall then fill such vacancies.

7.22 | ART 1 SEC 3 CL 2 | Ⓦ

Exemption of the Places of Choosing Senators from Regulation by Congress

[The times, places, and manner of holding elections for senators and representatives shall be prescribed in each state by the legislature thereof, but the Congress may at any time by law make or alter such regulations,]

except as to the places of choosing senators.*

7.23 | ART 1 SEC 4 CL 1 | Ⓢ

---

* The original Constitution did not give the national government power to regulate the places of choosing senators, because this would have been a power to control where the state legislatures met while they were choosing senators as provided by Clause 7.21. The reason for this phrase disappeared when the power to elect senators was transferred from the legislatures to the people by Clause 1.7.

Ⓦ Words repeated with changes by an amendment (implicitly repealed)

Ⓢ Subject matter abolished by an amendment (implicitly repealed)

Nonapplicability of the Requirement of Popular Election to Senators Chosen Before It Was Adopted

[The Senate of the United States shall be composed of two senators from each state, elected by the people thereof.]

This amendment shall not be so construed as to affect the election or term of any senator chosen before it becomes valid as part of the Constitution.

this amendment Clauses 1.7, 1.10, 7.24, and 7.36

7.24 | 17TH AMEND | Ⓟ

The President and Vice President
Election
The Electoral Votes
Voting by the Electors for Two Persons, Transmitting the Results

The electors shall meet in their respective states and vote by ballot for two persons, of whom one at least shall not be an inhabitant of the same state as themselves, and

they shall make a list of all the persons voted for and of the number of votes for each, which list they shall sign and certify and transmit sealed to the seat of the government of the United States, directed to the president of the Senate.

7.25 | ART 2 SEC 1 CL 3 | Ⓦ

Counting the Electoral Votes in Congress

The president of the Senate shall, in the presence of the Senate and House of Representatives, open all the certificates, and the votes shall then be counted.

7.26 | ART 2 SEC 1 CL 3 | Ⓦ

Ⓟ Served its purpose

Ⓦ Words repeated with changes by an amendment (implicitly repealed)

Election of the President

The Person Having the Most Electoral Votes, If These Are Equal to a Majority of the Electors, Becomes President

The person having the greatest number of votes shall be the President, if such number is a majority of the whole number of electors appointed.

7.27 | ART 2 SEC 1 CL 3 | Ⓦ

In Case of a Tie, or If No Person Has a Majority, the House of Representatives Chooses a President

If there are more than one who have such majority and have an equal number of votes, then the House of Representatives shall immediately choose by ballot one of them for President, and if no person has a majority, then from the five highest on the list the said House shall in like manner choose the President, but

in choosing the President the votes shall be taken by states, the representation from each state having one vote; a quorum for this purpose shall consist of a member or members from two-thirds of the states, and a majority of all the states shall be necessary to a choice.

7.28 | ART 2 SEC 1 CL 3 | Ⓦ

If No President Is Chosen Before March 4, the Vice President Acts As President

If the House of Representatives shall not choose a President whenever the right of choice shall devolve upon it, before the fourth day of March next following, then the Vice President shall act as President, as in the case of the death or other constitutional disability of the President.

7.29 | 12TH AMEND | Ⓦ

the fourth day of March the date on which the terms of the President, Vice President, and members of Congress began and ended, from 1789 until new dates were set by Clauses 1.14 and 1.46. The new dates became effective with the Congressional terms beginning in 1935 and the Presidential and Vice Presidential term beginning in 1937.

Ⓦ Words repeated with changes by an amendment (implicitly repealed)

Election of the Vice President
The Person Having the Most Electoral Votes,
After the Choice of a President, Becomes Vice President

In every case, after the choice of the President, the person having the greatest number of votes of the electors shall be the Vice President.

7.30 | ART 2 SEC 1 CL 3 | Ⓦ

In Case of a Tie the Senate Chooses a Vice President

But if there should remain two or more who have equal votes, the Senate shall choose from them by ballot the Vice President.

7.31 | ART 2 SEC 1 CL 3 | Ⓦ

The Powers and Duties of the Presidency Devolve on the Vice President

In case of the removal of the President from office or of his death, resignation, or inability to discharge the powers and duties of the said office, the same shall devolve on the Vice President.

7.32 | ART 2 SEC 1 CL 6 | Ⓦ

the powers and duties of the said office . . . shall devolve on the Vice President the Vice President shall be President (except that the meaning of this language in a case of Presidential disability was never decided while it was in force)

Nonapplicability of the Two-Term Limit to the President Holding Office When It Was Proposed, and to the Term in Which It Was Adopted

[No person shall be elected to the office of President more than twice.]

But this amendment shall not apply to any person holding the office of President when this amendment was proposed by the Congress,

this amendment Clauses 1.21, 7.33, and 8.7

and shall not prevent any person who may be holding the office of President, or acting as President, during the term within which this amendment becomes operative from holding the office of President or acting as President during the remainder of such term.

7.33 | 22ND AMEND SEC 1 | Ⓟ

Ⓟ Served its purpose

Ⓦ Words repeated with changes by an amendment (implicitly repealed)

Dates on Which Congress Assembles and Terms Begin

Congress Assembles in December

The Congress shall assemble at least once in every year, and such meeting shall be on the first Monday in December, unless the Congress shall by law appoint a different day.

7.34 | ART 1 SEC 4 CL 2 | Ⓦ

Making the Changeover to the New Dates on Which Terms Begin

[The terms of the President and Vice President shall end at noon on the twentieth day of January, and the terms of senators and representatives at noon on the third day of January,]

of the years in which such terms would have ended if this amendment had not been ratified,

this amendment Clauses 1.14, 1.33–1.36, 1.46, 1.50, 7.35, 8.4, and 8.5

[and the terms of their successors shall then begin].

7.35 | 20TH AMEND SEC 1 | Ⓟ

Rights

The Right to Vote

Qualifications for Voting for Representative and Senator Are the Same As for the Most Numerous Branch of the State Legislature

[The electors in each state shall have the qualifications requisite for electors of]

the most numerous branch* of

branch house, chamber (as used here)

[the state legislature].

7.36 | ART 1 SEC 2 CL 1 & 17TH AMEND | ◎

---

* This language was designed to prevent states from limiting the right to vote for Congress to a small group of voters, as a few states had done by allowing only land owners to vote for the state senate (the less numerous branch). No state has had different qualifications for voting for its two houses since the 1860s.

Ⓟ Served its purpose

Ⓦ Words repeated with changes by an amendment (implicitly repealed)

◎ Obsolete: the subject matter or situation has disappeared and is not likely to return

The Ban on Poll Taxes Is Limited to Voting for National Offices

[The right of citizens of the United States to vote in any primary or other election]

for President or Vice President, for electors for President or Vice President, or for senator or representative in Congress,*

[shall not be denied or abridged by the United States or any state by reason of failure to pay any poll tax or other tax].

7.37 | 24TH AMEND | ©

Rights in Court

Right to Trial by Jury in Suits at Common Law: Value in Controversy Must Exceed Twenty Dollars

[In suits at common law,]

where the value in controversy shall exceed twenty dollars,†

[the right of trial by jury shall be preserved].

7.38 | 7TH AMEND | ◎

---

* After this clause was adopted, the Supreme Court ruled that the poll tax violates the right to equal protection of the laws (Clause 5.2) and is unconstitutional, not just in elections to these offices in the national government, but in all elections.

† Twenty dollars is so small an amount that this restriction rarely, if ever, affected anyone's right to a trial by jury in a lawsuit, even in the early years of the Constitution. The fees charged for filing many kinds of lawsuits in courts of the United States are now much greater than this.

◎ Obsolete: the subject matter or situation has disappeared and is not likely to return

© A Supreme Court decision has established a broader right

Rights in Criminal Prosecutions: A Person May Be Prosecuted on a Presentment by a Grand Jury

[No person shall be held to answer for a capital or otherwise infamous crime, unless on an]

presentment* or

[indictment of a grand jury.]

7.39 | 5TH AMEND | ©

presentment (pri zent′mənt) a report by a grand jury; here, an accusation that a person has committed a crime, made by a grand jury on its own initiative and based on the members' own knowledge of the facts

Punishment of Treason: Ban on Corruption of Blood

No attainder of treason shall work corruption of blood,† or forfeiture except during the life of the person attainted.

7.40 | ART 3 SEC 3 CL 2 | ◎

attainder in old English law, a punishment that could accompany the death penalty, such as forfeiture of one's property

work cause (as used here)

forfeiture (for′ fi chər) the taking of a person's property by the government, as a result of the violation of a law

except during after

attainted convicted and punished

---

* Accusation by presentment, rather than indictment as provided in Clause 5.24, was always very rare, even in the early years. It has not been allowed since 1946, under the rules of criminal procedure of the courts of the United States, adopted by the Supreme Court.

† Corruption of blood was a part of the old English punishment of treason: after the condemned traitor's property was taken by (forfeited to) the king or queen and he (traitors usually being men) was executed, no line of descent or inheritance (bloodline) could be traced through him. Any property that would later have been inherited through him, for example by his son from his father, was instead forfeited.

　　Corruption of blood was abolished in Great Britain long ago, and it has never had a place in American ideas about crime and punishment.

◎ Obsolete: the subject matter or situation has disappeared and is not likely to return

© A rule of the United States courts, adopted by the Supreme Court, has established a broader protection

Other Provisions That Now Have No Effect

Land Claims

Claims of the United States and of the States

[The Congress shall have power to dispose of and make all needful rules and regulations respecting the territory or other property belonging to the United States;] and

nothing in this Constitution shall be so construed as to prejudice any claims* of the United States or of any particular state.

prejudice damage, prejudge

7.41 | ART 4 SEC 3 CL 2 | ◎

Claims of Citizens

[The judicial power shall extend . . . to controversies . . .]

between citizens of the same state claiming lands under grants of different states.

7.42 | ART 3 SEC 2 CL 1 | ◎

Letters of Marque and Reprisal

Power of the National Government to Grant

[The Congress shall have power to . . .]

grant letters of marque and reprisal.†

letters of marque (mark) **and reprisal** documents authorizing privately owned armed ships (privateers) to attack and capture the merchant ships of an enemy nation

7.43 | ART 1 SEC 8 CL 11 | ◎

---

* The last of the original states' claims to western lands were given over to the national government shortly after the Constitution was adopted. Claims of individuals to these lands and disputes over the original state boundary lines were settled in the years that followed.

† Privateering was made obsolete by the arrival of the steam warship, which was fast, armored, heavily armed, and very expensive. Most seafaring nations renounced the practice in the mid-19th century. Letters of marque and reprisal were last issued by the United States government in the War of 1812.

◎ Obsolete: the subject matter or situation has disappeared and is not likely to return

Ban on Granting by the States

[No state shall . . .]

grant letters of marque and reprisal.

7.44 | ART 1 SEC 10 CL 1 | Ⓞ

Prohibition of the Manufacture, Sale, Transportation, Importation, and Exportation of Intoxicating Liquors

Prohibition

The manufacture, sale, or transportation of intoxicating liquors within; the importation thereof into; or the exportation thereof from the United States and all territory subject to the jurisdiction thereof for beverage purposes is hereby prohibited.

The Congress and the several states shall have concurrent power to enforce this amendment by appropriate legislation.

7.45 | 18TH AMEND SECS 1 & 2 | Ⓡ

concurrent acting together

this amendment Clauses 7.45, 8.2, and 8.3

Repeal of Prohibition

The eighteenth amendment to the Constitution of the United States is hereby repealed.

7.46 | 21ST AMEND SEC 1 | Ⓟ

the eighteenth amendment to the Constitution Clauses 7.45, 8.2, and 8.3

hereby by this

repealed revoked, removed from the Constitution

Ⓟ Served its purpose

Ⓡ Repealed by an amendment

Ⓞ Obsolete: the subject matter or situation has disappeared and is not likely to return

Chapter 8
Procedures of Adoption

Procedure for Adopting the Original Constitution

The ratification of the conventions of nine states shall be sufficient for the establishment of this Constitution between the states so ratifying the same.

8.1 | ART 7

Amendments: Effective Dates, Methods of Ratification, Time Limits

The 18th Amendment (Prohibition of Intoxicating Liquors)

Effective Date

After one year from the ratification of this article,

[the manufacture, sale, or transportation of intoxicating liquors . . . for beverage purposes is hereby prohibited.]*

8.2 | 18TH AMEND SEC 1

PROCEDURES OF ADOPTION
The final clauses (8.1–8.7) contain the language that set forth procedures for adoption of the original Constitution and some of the amendments. These clauses have served their purposes. Each clause applied only to one specific adoption process—the general rules for adoption of amendments are given in Clauses 6.1–6.3.

one year from the ratification of this article January 16, 1920

article a part of a document, an amendment (as used here)

---

* In this clause, the language shown in brackets has been repealed like the non-bracketed language, as is shown in Clause 7.46.

Method of Ratification, Time Limit on Adoption

This article shall be inoperative unless it shall have been ratified as an amendment to the Constitution by the legislatures of the several states, as provided in the Constitution, within seven years from the date of the submission hereof to the states by the Congress.

inoperative lacking effect, no longer a proposed amendment to the Constitution

hereof of this

8.3 | 18TH AMEND SEC 3

The 20th Amendment (Beginning of Terms, Time of Assembling, Filling Vacancies)

Effective Date of the New Beginnings of Terms and Time of Assembling

Sections 1 and 2 shall take effect on the fifteenth day of October following the ratification of this article.

sections 1 and 2 Clauses 1.14, 1.46, and 1.50

the fifteenth day of October following the ratification of this article October 15, 1933

8.4 | 20TH AMEND SEC 5

Method of Ratification, Time Limit on Adoption

This article shall be inoperative unless it shall have been ratified as an amendment to the Constitution by the legislatures of three-fourths of the several states within seven years from the date of its submission.

8.5 | 20TH AMEND SEC 6

The 21st Amendment (Repeal of Prohibition)

Method of Ratification, Time Limit on Adoption

This article shall be inoperative unless it shall have been ratified as an amendment to the Constitution by conventions in the several states, as provided in the Constitution, within seven years from the date of the submission hereof to the states by the Congress.

8.6 | 21ST AMEND SEC 3

The 22nd Amendment
(Two-Term Limit on the President)

Method of Ratification, Time Limit on Adoption

This article shall be inoperative unless it shall have been ratified as an amendment to the Constitution by the legislatures of three-fourths of the several states within seven years from the date of its submission to the states by the Congress.

8.7 | 22ND AMEND SEC 2

Chapter 9
Actions Proposing the Constitution and Amendments

Document Presenting the Original Constitution

The Proposed Constitution

[Text of the original Constitution]

Testimonium Clause

Done in Convention, by the unanimous consent of the states present, the seventeenth day of September, in the year of our Lord one thousand seven hundred and eighty-seven, and of the Independence of the United States of America the twelfth.

ACTIONS PROPOSING ADOPTION

The Modern Edition concludes with some text that is not part of the Constitution but shows the actions by which the original Constitution and some amendments were proposed. This text comprises the "Done in Convention" language and the names of the members of the Constitutional Convention who signed the document, and the joint resolutions by which Congress has proposed amendments, signed by the presiding officers of the two houses.

testimonium clause the final clause of a document, giving the date and followed by signatures

Signers

In witness whereof we have hereunto subscribed our names.

hereunto to this

subscribe write below

George Washington, *President and Deputy from Virginia*

deputy delegate, representative (as used here)

New Hampshire
John Langdon
Nicholas Gilman

Massachusetts
Nathaniel Gorham
Rufus King

Connecticut
William Samuel Johnson
Roger Sherman

New York
Alexander Hamilton

New Jersey
William Livingston
David Brearley
William Paterson
Jonathan Dayton

Pennsylvania
Benjamin Franklin
Thomas Mifflin
Robert Morris
George Clymer
Thomas Fitzsimons
Jared Ingersoll
James Wilson
Gouverneur Morris

Delaware
George Read
Gunning Bedford, Jr.
John Dickinson
Richard Bassett
Jacob Broom

Maryland
James McHenry
Daniel of St. Thomas
 Jenifer
Daniel Carroll

Virginia
John Blair
James Madison, Jr.

North Carolina
William Blount
Richard Dobbs Spaight
Hugh Williamson

South Carolina
John Rutledge
Charles Cotesworth
 Pinckney
Charles Pinckney
Pierce Butler

Georgia
William Few
Abraham Baldwin

Attest: William Jackson, *Secretary*

ACTION OF THE CONVENTION, SEPTEMBER 17, 1787

attest certify that a document is accurate or genuine

Joint Resolution of the First Congress Proposing Twelve Amendments

Preamble

The conventions of a number of the states having at the time of their adopting the Constitution expressed a desire, in order to prevent misconstruction or abuse of its powers, that further declaratory and restrictive clauses should be added, and as extending the ground of public confidence in the government will best insure the beneficent ends of its institution;

misconstruction incorrect interpretation

its powers the powers that it gives to the national government

extending the ground broadening the base

insure the beneficent (bə nef′ i sənt) **ends of its institution** assure the good purposes of its adoption—see the Preamble

Resolving Clause

Resolved by the Senate and House of Representatives of the United States of America in Congress assembled, two-thirds of both houses concurring,

that the following articles be proposed to the legislatures of the several states as amendments to the Constitution of the United States, all or any of which articles, when ratified by three-fourths of the said legislatures, to be valid to all intents and purposes as parts of the said Constitution:

Heading

Articles in addition to and amendment of the Constitution of the United States of America, proposed by Congress and ratified by the legislatures of the several states, pursuant to the fifth article of the original Constitution.

pursuant to conforming to, in accordance with

The Proposed Amendments

[Text of twelve proposed amendments: the first ten amendments, the 27th Amendment, and one amendment that was not adopted]

Signers

Frederick Augustus Muhlenberg
Speaker of the House of Representatives

John Adams
Vice President of the United States
and President of the Senate

Attest, John Beckley
Clerk of the House of Representatives

Samuel A. Otis
Secretary of the Senate

JOINT RESOLUTION OF CONGRESS, SEPTEMBER 25, 1789

Joint Resolution of the 92nd Congress Proposing the 26th Amendment *

Resolving Clause

Resolved by the Senate and House of Representatives of the United States of America in Congress assembled (two-thirds of each house concurring therein),

That the following article is proposed as an amendment to the Constitution of the United States, which shall be valid to all intents and purposes as part of the Constitution when ratified by the legislatures of three-fourths of the several states within seven years from the date of its submission by the Congress:

The Proposed Amendment

[Text of the proposed amendment]

---

* The amendments since the Bill of Rights have been proposed by joint resolutions of Congress having approximately this form. (In proposing the 21st Amendment—Clauses 2.11, 7.46, and 8.6—Congress called for ratification by conventions in the states, not by the legislatures.)

Some of the joint resolutions, including this one, have set a time limit for the adoption process, while some others (Clauses 8.3 and 8.5–8.7) have placed a limit in the amendment itself.

Signers

Carl Albert
Speaker of the House of Representatives

Allen J. Ellender
President of the Senate pro Tempore

I certify that this joint resolution
originated in the Senate.*

Francis R. Valeo
Secretary

JOINT RESOLUTION OF CONGRESS, MARCH 23, 1971

---

* When both houses of Congress pass a bill, or a resolution requiring the President's approval, a notation like this is added to show
which house the document should be returned to if the President does not approve it, as provided by Clauses 1.60 and 1.62.
When Congress proposes an amendment to the Constitution,
such a notation is usually included on the joint resolution, though
it serves no purpose since the President's approval is not needed.

THE TRADITIONAL ARRANGEMENT OF THE CONSTITUTION

THE TRADITIONAL ARRANGEMENT OF THE CONSTITUTION

The different parts of the Constitution are traditionally arranged in the order of their adoption: the original Constitution, adopted in 1788, followed by the Bill of Rights in 1791 and the later amendments at various dates beginning in 1795.

You will find the Traditional Arrangement helpful when you read about the Constitution in other sources and come across references to particular articles and amendments—as in "Article III judges" or "First-Amendment freedoms"—and need to know precisely what these contain.

Many modern printings of the Traditional Arrangement give faithful copies of the engrossed (handwritten) copy of the original Constitution, signed by 39 members of the Convention, and the engrossed copy of the Bill of Rights as proposed by Congress. These display an annoying feature of the handiwork of eighteenth-century scribes—many common nouns begin with capital letters, lending a distinctly antique appearance to the text.

In this book we offer a more modern-looking text of the Traditional Arrangement by copying early printings of the Constitution, which have very few capital letters. (We have added clause numbers.)

- **The original Constitution.** Our text is taken from the copy that was produced by Philadelphia printers Dunlap and Claypoole, at the order of the Constitutional Convention, late on September 17, 1787, and was carried away on the next day by the departing delegates, to be reproduced by printers in their states and by the printer of the Confederation Congress.

- **The first ten amendments.** We copy the text of the amendments that was published by Secretary of State Thomas Jefferson when he announced that they had been ratified.

- **The later amendments.** We copy each amendment as it was produced by the printers serving the government at the time of the amendment's adoption. Starting in the twentieth century, the printer is the Government Printing Office.

By using early printed copies as our models, we give today's readers a printing of the original Constitution and the early amendments that is very much like what people were accustomed to reading during the Constitution's first 60 years (nearly until the Civil War). In those times almost all printed copies of the Constitution followed the first prints rather than the engrossed copies.

The subsequent shift from the printed to the engrossed model resulted from the government's failure to keep and distribute certified booklet copies of the official print of 1787. As time passed, publishers tended to copy any available print, so a few small errors in the early prints were gradually mutliplied. Finally, to produce an error-free copy it was necessary to go back to the engrossed original of 1787, which was proved to be authentic by the signatures of Washington, Madison, and the other delegates.

The Original Constitution

Preamble WE, the People of the United States, in order to form a more perfect union, establish justice, insure domestic tranquility, provide for the common defence, promote the general welfare, and secure the blessings of liberty to ourselves and our posterity, do ordain and establish this Constitution for the United States of America.

Article I *Section 1.* ALL legislative powers herein granted shall be vested in a Congress of the United States, which shall consist of a Senate and House of Representatives.

Section 2. [1] The House of Representatives shall be composed of members chosen every second year by the people of the several states, and the electors in each state shall have the qualifications requisite for electors of the most numerous branch of the state legislature.

[2] No person shall be a representative who shall not have attained to the age of twenty-five years, and been seven years

a citizen of the United States, and who shall not, when elected, be an inhabitant of that state in which he shall be chosen.

³ Representatives and direct taxes shall be apportioned among the several states which may be included within this Union, according to their respective numbers, which shall be determined by adding to the whole number of free persons, including those bound to service for a term of years, and excluding Indians not taxed, three-fifths of all other persons. The actual enumeration shall be made within three years after the first meeting of the Congress of the United States, and within every subsequent term of ten years, in such manner as they shall by law direct. The number of representatives shall not exceed one for every thirty thousand, but each state shall have at least one representative; and until such enumeration shall be made, the state of New-Hampshire shall be entitled to chuse three, Massachusetts eight, Rhode-Island and Providence Plantations one, Connecticut five, New-York six, New-Jersey four, Pennsylvania eight, Delaware one, Maryland six, Virginia ten, North-Carolina five, South-Carolina five, and Georgia three.

⁴ When vacancies happen in the representation from any state, the Executive authority thereof shall issue writs of election to fill such vacancies.

⁵ The House of Representatives shall chuse their Speaker and other officers; and shall have the sole power of impeachment.

Section 3. ¹ The Senate of the United States shall be composed of two senators from each state, chosen by the legislature thereof, for six years; and each senator shall have one vote.

² Immediately after they shall be assembled in consequence of the first election, they shall be divided as equally as may be into three classes. The seats of the senators of the first class shall be vacated at the expiration of the second year, of the second class at the expiration of the fourth year, and of the third class at the expiration of the sixth year, so that one-third may be chosen every second year; and if vacancies happen by resignation, or otherwise, during the recess of the Legislature of any state, the Executive thereof may make temporary appoint-

ments until the next meeting of the Legislature, which shall then fill such vacancies.

[3] No person shall be a senator who shall not have attained to the age of thirty years, and been nine years a citizen of the United States, and who shall not, when elected, be an inhabitant of that state for which he shall be chosen.

[4] The Vice-President of the United States shall be President of the senate, but shall have no vote, unless they be equally divided.

[5] The Senate shall chuse their other officers, and also a President pro tempore, in the absence of the Vice-President, or when he shall exercise the office of President of the United States.

[6] The Senate shall have the sole power to try all impeachments. When sitting for that purpose, they shall be on oath or affirmation. When the President of the United States is tried, the Chief Justice shall preside: And no person shall be convicted without the concurrence of two-thirds of the members present.

[7] Judgment in cases of impeachment shall not extend further than to removal from office, and disqualification to hold and enjoy any office of honor, trust or profit under the United States; but the party convicted shall nevertheless be liable and subject to indictment, trial, judgment and punishment, according to law.

Section 4. [1] The times, places and manner of holding elections for senators and representatives, shall be prescribed in each state by the legislature thereof; but the Congress may at any time by law make or alter such regulations, except as to the places of chusing Senators.

[2] The Congress shall assemble at least once in every year, and such meeting shall be on the first Monday in December, unless they shall by law appoint a different day.

Section 5. [1] Each house shall be the judge of the elections, returns and qualifications of its own members, and a majority of each shall constitute a quorum to do business; but a smaller number may adjourn from day to day, and may be authorized to compel the attendance of absent members, in such manner, and under such penalties as each house may provide.

² Each house may determine the rules of its proceedings, punish its members for disorderly behaviour, and, with the concurrence of two-thirds, expel a member.

³ Each house shall keep a journal of its proceedings, and from time to time publish the same, excepting such parts as may in their judgment require secrecy; and the yeas and nays of the members of either house on any question shall, at the desire of one-fifth of those present, be entered on the journal.

⁴ Neither house, during the session of Congress, shall, without the consent of the other, adjourn for more than three days, nor to any other place than that in which the two houses shall be sitting.

Section 6. ¹ The senators and representatives shall receive a compensation for their services, to be ascertained by law, and paid out of the treasury of the United States. They shall in all cases, except treason, felony and breach of the peace, be privileged from arrest during their attendance at the session of their respective houses, and in going to and returning from the same; and for any speech or debate in either house, they shall not be questioned in any other place.

² No senator or representative shall, during the time for which he was elected, be appointed to any civil office under the authority of the United States, which shall have been created, or the emoluments whereof shall have been increased during such time; and no person holding any office under the United States, shall be a member of either house during his continuance in office.

Section 7. ¹ All bills for raising revenue shall originate in the house of representatives; but the senate may propose or concur with amendments as on other bills.

² Every bill which shall have passed the house of representatives and the senate, shall, before it become a law, be presented to the president of the United States; if he approve he shall sign it, but if not he shall return it, with his objections to that house in which it shall have originated, who shall enter the objections

at large on their journal, and proceed to reconsider it. If after such reconsideration two-thirds of that house shall agree to pass the bill, it shall be sent, together with the objections, to the other house, by which it shall likewise be reconsidered, and if approved by two-thirds of that house, it shall become a law. But in all such cases the votes of both houses shall be determined by yeas and nays, and the names of the persons voting for and against the bill shall be entered on the journal of each house respectively. If any bill shall not be returned by the President within ten days (Sundays excepted) after it shall have been presented to him, the same shall be a law, in like manner as if he had signed it, unless the Congress by their adjournment prevent its return, in which case it shall not be a law.

³ Every order, resolution, or vote to which the concurrence of the Senate and House of Representatives may be necessary (except on a question of adjournment) shall be presented to the President of the United States; and before the same shall take effect, shall be approved by him, or, being disapproved by him, shall be repassed by two-thirds of the Senate and House of Representatives, according to the rules and limitations prescribed in the case of a bill.

Section 8. The Congress shall have power
¹ To lay and collect taxes, duties, imposts and excises, to pay the debts and provide for the common defence and general welfare of the United States; but all duties, imposts and excises shall be uniform throughout the United States;

² To borrow money on the credit of the United States;

³ To regulate commerce with foreign nations, and among the several states, and with the Indian tribes;

⁴ To establish an uniform rule of naturalization, and uniform laws on the subject of bankruptcies throughout the United States;

⁵ To coin money, regulate the value thereof, and of foreign coin, and fix the standard of weights and measures;

⁶ To provide for the punishment of counterfeiting the securities and current coin of the United States;

⁷ To establish post offices and post roads;

⁸ To promote the progress of science and useful arts, by securing for limited times to authors and inventors the exclusive right to their respective writings and discoveries;

⁹ To constitute tribunals inferior to the supreme court;

¹⁰ To define and punish piracies and felonies committed on the high seas, and offences against the law of nations;

¹¹ To declare war, grant letters of marque and reprisal, and make rules concerning captures on land and water;

¹² To raise and support armies, but no appropriation of money to that use shall be for a longer term than two years;

¹³ To provide and maintain a navy;

¹⁴ To make rules for the government and regulation of the land and naval forces;

¹⁵ To provide for calling forth the militia to execute the laws of the union, suppress insurrections and repel invasions;

¹⁶ To provide for organizing, arming, and disciplining, the militia, and for governing such part of them as may be employed in the service of the United States, reserving to the States respectively, the appointment of the officers, and the authority of training the militia according to the discipline prescribed by Congress;

¹⁷ To exercise exclusive legislation in all cases whatsoever, over such district (not exceeding ten miles square) as may, by cession of particular States, and the acceptance of Congress, become the seat of the government of the United States, and to exercise like authority over all places purchased by the consent of the legislature of the state in which the same shall be, for the erection of forts, magazines, arsenals, dockyards, and other needful buildings;—And

¹⁸ To make all laws which shall be necessary and proper for carrying into execution the foregoing powers, and all other powers vested by this constitution in the government of the United States, or in any department or officer thereof.

Section 9. ¹ The migration or importation of such persons as any of the states now existing shall think proper to admit, shall not be prohibited by the Congress prior to the year one thousand eight hundred and eight, but a tax or duty may be imposed on such importation, not exceeding ten dollars for each person.

² The privilege of the writ of habeas corpus shall not be suspended, unless when in cases of rebellion or invasion the public safety may require it.

³ No bill of attainder or ex post facto law shall be passed.

⁴ No capitation, or other direct, tax shall be laid, unless in proportion to the census or enumeration hereinbefore directed to be taken.

⁵ No tax or duty shall be laid on articles exported from any state.

⁶ No preference shall be given by any regulation of commerce or revenue to the ports of one state over those of another: nor shall vessels bound to, or from, one state, be obliged to enter, clear, or pay duties in another.

⁷ No money shall be drawn from the treasury, but in consequence of appropriations made by law; and a regular statement and account of the receipts and expenditures of all public money shall be published from time to time.

⁸ No title of nobility shall be granted by the United States:— And no person holding any office of profit or trust under them, shall, without the consent of the Congress, accept of any present, emolument, office, or title, of any kind whatever, from any king, prince, or foreign state.

Section 10. ¹ No state shall enter into any treaty, alliance, or confederation; grant letters of marque and reprisal; coin money; emit bills of credit; make any thing but gold and silver coin a tender in payment of debts; pass any bill of attainder, ex post facto law, or law impairing the obligation of contracts, or grant any title of nobility.

² No state shall, without the consent of the Congress, lay any imposts or duties on imports or exports, except what may be absolutely necessary for executing its inspection laws; and the net produce of all duties and imposts, laid by any state on imports or exports, shall be for the use of the Treasury of the United States; and all such laws shall be subject to the revision and controul of the Congress.

³ No state shall, without the consent of Congress, lay any duty of tonnage, keep troops, or ships of war in time of peace, enter into any agreement or compact with another state, or with

a foreign power, or engage in war, unless actually invaded, or in such imminent danger as will not admit of delay.

Article II   *Section 1.* [1] The executive power shall be vested in a president of the United States of America. He shall hold his office during the term of four years, and, together with the vice-president, chosen for the same term, be elected as follows.

[2] Each state shall appoint, in such manner as the legislature thereof may direct, a number of electors, equal to the whole number of senators and representatives to which the state may be entitled in the Congress: but no senator or representative, or person holding an office of trust or profit under the United States, shall be appointed an elector.

[3] The electors shall meet in their respective states, and vote by ballot for two persons, of whom one at least shall not be an inhabitant of the same state with themselves. And they shall make a list of all the persons voted for, and of the number of votes for each; which list they shall sign and certify, and transmit sealed to the seat of the government of the United States, directed to the president of the senate. The president of the senate shall, in the presence of the senate and house of representatives, open all the certificates, and the votes shall then be counted. The person having the greatest number of votes shall be the president, if such number be a majority of the whole number of electors appointed; and if there be more than one who have such majority, and have an equal number of votes, then the house of representatives shall immediately chuse by ballot one of them for president; and if no person have a majority, then from the five highest on the list the said house shall in like manner chuse the president. But in chusing the president, the votes shall be taken by states, the representation from each state having one vote; a quorum for this purpose shall consist of a member or members from two-thirds of the states, and a majority of all the states shall be necessary to a choice. In every case, after the choice of the president, the person having the greatest number of votes of the electors shall be the vice-president. But if there should remain two or

more who have equal votes, the senate shall chuse from them by ballot the vice-president.

⁴ The Congress may determine the time of chusing the electors, and the day on which they shall give their votes; which day shall be the same throughout the United States.

⁵ No person except a natural born citizen, or a citizen of the United States, at the time of the adoption of this constitution, shall be eligible to the office of president; neither shall any person be eligible to that office who shall not have attained to the age of thirty-five years, and been fourteen years a resident within the United States.

⁶ In case of the removal of the president from office, or of his death, resignation, or inability to discharge the powers and duties of the said office, the same shall devolve on the vice-president, and the Congress may by law provide for the case of removal, death, resignation or inability, both of the president and vice-president, declaring what officer shall then act as president, and such officer shall act accordingly, until the disability be removed, or a president shall be elected.

⁷ The president shall, at stated times, receive for his services, a compensation, which shall neither be increased nor diminished during the period for which he shall have been elected, and he shall not receive within that period any other emolument from the United States, or any of them.

⁸ Before he enter on the execution of his office, he shall take the following oath or affirmation: "I do solemnly swear (or affirm) that I will faithfully execute the office of president of the United States, and will to the best of my ability, preserve, protect and defend the constitution of the United States."

Section 2. ¹ The president shall be commander in chief of the army and navy of the United States, and of the militia of the several States, when called into the actual service of the United States; he may require the opinion, in writing, of the principal officer in each of the executive departments, upon any subject relating to the duties of their respective offices, and he shall have power to grant reprieves and pardons for offences against the United States, except in cases of impeachment.

² He shall have power, by and with the advice and consent of the senate, to make treaties, provided two-thirds of the senators present concur; and he shall nominate, and by and with the advice and consent of the senate, shall appoint ambassadors, other public ministers and consuls, judges of the supreme court, and all other officers of the United States, whose appointments are not herein otherwise provided for, and which shall be established by law. But the Congress may by law vest the appointment of such inferior officers, as they think proper, in the president alone, in the courts of law, or in the heads of departments.

³ The president shall have power to fill up all vacancies that may happen during the recess of the senate, by granting commissions which shall expire at the end of their next session.

Section 3. He shall from time to time give to the Congress information of the state of the union, and recommend to their consideration such measures as he shall judge necessary and expedient; he may, on extraordinary occasions, convene both houses, or either of them, and in case of disagreement between them, with respect to the time of adjournment, he may adjourn them to such time as he shall think proper; he shall receive ambassadors and other public ministers; he shall take care that the laws be faithfully executed, and shall commission all the officers of the United States.

Section 4. The president, vice-president and all civil officers of the United States, shall be removed from office on impeachment for, and conviction of, treason, bribery, or other high crimes and misdemeanors.

Article III   *Section 1.* The judicial power of the United States, shall be vested in one supreme court, and in such inferior courts as the Congress may from time to time ordain and establish. The judges, both of the supreme and inferior courts, shall hold their offices during good behaviour, and shall, at stated times, receive for their services, a compensation, which shall not be diminished during their continuance in office.

Section 2. [1] The judicial power shall extend to all cases, in law and equity, arising under this constitution, the laws of the United States, and treaties made, or which shall be made, under their authority; to all cases affecting ambassadors, other public ministers and consuls; to all cases of admiralty and maritime jurisdiction; to controversies to which the United States shall be a party; to controversies between two or more States, between a state and citizens of another state, between citizens of different States, between citizens of the same state claiming lands under grants of different States, and between a state, or the citizens thereof, and foreign States, citizens or subjects.

[2] In all cases affecting ambassadors, other public ministers and consuls, and those in which a state shall be party, the supreme court shall have original jurisdiction. In all the other cases before mentioned, the supreme court shall have appellate jurisdiction, both as to law and fact, with such exceptions, and under such regulations as the Congress shall make.

[3] The trial of all crimes, except in cases of impeachment, shall be by jury; and such trial shall be held in the state where the said crimes shall have been committed; but when not committed within any state, the trial shall be at such place or places as the Congress may by law have directed.

Section 3. [1] Treason against the United States, shall consist only in levying war against them, or in adhering to their enemies, giving them aid and comfort. No person shall be convicted of treason unless on the testimony of two witnesses to the same overt act, or on confession in open court.

[2] The Congress shall have power to declare the punishment of treason, but no attainder of treason shall work corruption of blood, or forfeiture except during the life of the person attainted.

Article IV   *Section 1.* Full faith and credit shall be given in each state to the public acts, records, and judicial proceedings of every other state.

And the Congress may by general laws prescribe the manner in which such acts, records and proceedings shall be proved, and the effect thereof.

Section 2. [1] The citizens of each state shall be entitled to all privileges and immunities of citizens in the several states.

[2] A person charged in any state with treason, felony, or other crime, who shall flee from justice, and be found in another state, shall, on demand of the executive authority of the state from which he fled, be delivered up, to be removed to the state having jurisdiction of the crime.

[3] No person held to service or labour in one state, under the laws thereof, escaping into another, shall, in consequence of any law or regulation therein, be discharged from such service or labour, but shall be delivered up on claim of the party to whom such service or labour may be due.

Section 3. [1] New states may be admitted by the Congress into this union; but no new state shall be formed or erected within the jurisdiction of any other state; nor any state be formed by the junction of two or more states, or parts of states, without the consent of the legislatures of the states concerned as well as of the Congress.

[2] The Congress shall have power to dispose of and make all needful rules and regulations respecting the territory or other property belonging to the United States; and nothing in this Constitution shall be so construed as to prejudice any claims of the United States, or of any particular state.

Section 4. The United States shall guarantee to every state in this union a Republican form of government, and shall protect each of them against invasion; and on application of the legislature, or of the executive (when the legislature cannot be convened) against domestic violence.

Article V   The Congress, whenever two-thirds of both houses shall deem it necessary, shall propose amendments to this constitution, or, on the application of the legislatures of two-thirds of the several states, shall call a convention for proposing amendments, which, in either case, shall be valid to all intents and purposes, as part of this constitution, when ratified by the legislatures of three-fourths of the several states, or by conventions in three-fourths thereof, as the one or the other mode of ratification may be proposed by the Congress; Provided, that no amendment which may be made prior to the year one thousand eight hundred and eight shall in any manner affect the first and fourth clauses in the ninth section of the first article; and that no state, without its consent, shall be deprived of its equal suffrage in the senate.

Article VI   [1] All debts contracted and engagements entered into, before the adoption of this Constitution, shall be as valid against the United States under this Constitution, as under the confederation.

[2] This constitution, and the laws of the United States which shall be made in pursuance thereof; and all treaties made, or which shall be made, under the authority of the United States, shall be the supreme law of the land; and the judges in every state shall be bound thereby, any thing in the constitution or laws of any state to the contrary notwithstanding.

[3] The senators and representatives beforementioned, and the members of the several state legislatures, and all executive and judicial officers, both of the United States and of the several States, shall be bound by oath or affirmation, to support this constitution; but no religious test shall ever be required as a qualification to any office or public trust under the United States.

Article VII   The ratification of the conventions of nine States, shall be sufficient for the establishment of this constitution between the States so ratifying the same.

The Bill of Rights

Amendment I   Congress shall make no law respecting an establishment of religion, or prohibiting the free exercise thereof, or abridging the freedom of speech, or of the press; or the right of the people peaceably to assemble, and to petition the government for a redress of grievances.

Amendment II   A well regulated militia being necessary to the security of a free state, the right of the people to keep and bear arms shall not be infringed.

Amendment III   No soldier shall in time of peace be quartered in any house without the consent of the owner; nor in time of war, but in a manner to be prescribed by law.

Amendment IV   The right of the people to be secure in their persons, houses, papers, and effects, against unreasonable searches and seizures, shall not be violated; and no warrants shall issue, but upon probable cause, supported by oath or affirmation, and particularly describing the place to be searched, and the persons or things to be seized.

Amendment V   No person shall be held to answer for a capital, or otherwise infamous crime, unless on a presentment or indictment of a grand jury, except in cases arising in the land or naval forces, or in the militia when in actual service in time of war or public danger; nor shall any person be subject for the same offense to be twice put in jeopardy of life or limb; nor shall be compelled in any criminal case to be a witness against himself, nor be deprived of life, liberty or property, without due process of law; nor shall private property be taken for public use without just compensation.

Amendment VI   In all criminal prosecutions the accused shall enjoy the right to a speedy and public trial, by an impartial jury of the state and district wherein the crime shall have been committed, which district shall have been previously ascertained by law, and to be informed of the nature and cause of the accusation; to be confronted with the witnesses against him; to have compulsory process for obtaining witnesses in his favor, and to have the assistance of counsel for his defense.

Amendment VII   In suits at common law, where the value in controversy shall exceed twenty dollars, the right of trial by jury shall be preserved; and no fact, tried by a jury, shall be otherwise re-examined in any court of the United States, than according to the rules of the common law.

Amendment VIII   Excessive bail shall not be required, nor excessive fines imposed, nor cruel and unusual punishments inflicted.

Amendment IX   The enumeration in the Constitution, of certain rights, shall not be construed to deny or disparage others retained by the people.

Amendment X   The powers not delegated to the United States by the Constitution, nor prohibited by it to the States, are reserved to the States respectively, or to the people.

The Later Amendments

Amendment XI   The judicial power of the United States shall not be construed to extend to any suit in law or equity, commenced or prosecuted against one of the United States by citizens of another state, or by citizens or subjects of any foreign state.

Amendment XII   The electors shall meet in their respective states, and vote by ballot for President and Vice President, one of whom, at least, shall not be an inhabitant of the same state with themselves; they shall name in their ballots the person voted for as President, and in distinct ballots the person voted for as Vice President; and they shall make distinct lists of all persons voted for as President, and of all persons voted for as Vice President, and of the number of votes for each, which lists they shall sign and certify, and transmit sealed to the seat of the government of the United States, directed to the President of the Senate; the President of the Senate shall, in the presence of the Senate and House of Representatives, open all the certificates, and the votes shall then be counted: the person having the greatest number of votes for President, shall be the President, if such number be a majority of the whole number of electors appointed; and if no person have such majority, then from the persons having the highest numbers not exceeding three on the list of those voted for as President, the House of Representatives shall choose immediately, by ballot, the President. But in choosing the President, the votes shall be taken by states, the representation from each state having one vote; a quorum for this purpose shall consist of a member or members from two thirds of the states, and a majority of all the states shall be necessary to a choice. And if the House of Representatives shall not choose a President whenever the right of choice shall devolve upon them, before the fourth day of March next following, then the Vice President shall act as President, as in the case of the death or other constitutional disability of the President.

The person having the greatest number of votes as Vice President, shall be the Vice President, if such number be a majority of the whole number of electors appointed; and if no person have a majority, then from the two highest numbers on the list, the Senate shall choose the Vice President: a quorum for the purpose shall consist of two-thirds of the whole number of senators, and a majority of the whole number shall be necessary to a choice.

But no person constitutionally ineligible to the office of President shall be eligible to that of Vice President of the United States.

Amendment XIII   *Section 1.* Neither slavery nor involuntary servitude, except as a punishment for crime whereof the party shall have been duly convicted, shall exist within the United States, or any place subject to their jurisdiction.

Section 2. Congress shall have power to enforce this article by appropriate legislation.

Amendment XIV   *Section 1.* All persons born or naturalized in the United States, and subject to the jurisdiction thereof, are citizens of the United States and of the State wherein they reside. No State shall make or enforce any law which shall abridge the privileges or immunities of citizens of the United States; nor shall any State deprive any person of life, liberty, or property, without due process of law, nor deny to any person within its jurisdiction the equal protection of the laws.

Section 2. Representatives shall be apportioned among the several States according to their respective numbers, counting the whole number of persons in each State, excluding Indians not taxed. But when the right to vote at any election for the choice of electors for President and Vice President of the United States, Representatives in Congress, the executive and judicial officers of a State, or the members of the legislature thereof, is denied to any of the male inhabitants of such State, being twenty-one years of age, and citizens of the United States, or in any way abridged, except for participation in rebellion or other crime, the basis of representation therein shall be reduced in the proportion which the number of such male citizens shall bear to the whole number of male citizens twenty-one years of age in such State.

Section 3. No person shall be a Senator or Representative in Congress, or elector of President and Vice President, or hold any office, civil or military, under the United States, or under any State, who, having previously taken an oath, as a member of Congress, or as an officer of the United States, or as a member of any State Legislature, or as an executive or judicial officer of any State, to support the Constitution of the United States, shall have engaged in insurrection or rebellion against the same, or given aid or comfort to the enemies thereof. But Congress may, by a vote of two-thirds of each House, remove such disability.

Section 4. The validity of the public debt of the United States, authorized by law, including debts incurred for payment of pensions and bounties for services in suppressing insurrection or rebellion, shall not be questioned. But neither the United States nor any State shall assume or pay any debt or obligation incurred in aid of insurrection or rebellion against the United States, or any claim for the loss or emancipation of any slave; but all such debts, obligations, and claims shall be held illegal and void.

Section 5. The Congress shall have power to enforce, by appropriate legislation, the provisions of this article.

Amendment XV

Section 1. The right of citizens of the United States to vote shall not be denied or abridged by the United States or by any State on account of race, color, or previous condition of servitude.

Section 2. The Congress shall have power to enforce this article by appropriate legislation.

Amendment XVI

The Congress shall have power to lay and collect taxes on incomes, from whatever source derived, without apportionment among the several States, and without regard to any census or enumeration.

Amendment XVII

The Senate of the United States shall be composed of two Senators from each State, elected by the people thereof, for six years; and each Senator shall have one vote. The electors in each State shall have the qualifications requisite for electors of the most numerous branch of the State legislatures.

When vacancies happen in the representation of any State in the Senate, the executive authority of such State shall issue writs of election to fill such vacancies: *Provided,* That the legislature of any State may empower the executive thereof to make temporary appointments until the people fill the vacancies by election as the legislature may direct.

This amendment shall not be so construed as to affect the election or term of any Senator chosen before it becomes valid as part of the Constitution.

Amendment XVIII   *Section 1.* After one year from the ratification of this article the manufacture, sale, or transportation of intoxicating liquors within, the importation thereof into, or the exportation thereof from the United States and all territory subject to the jurisdiction thereof for beverage purposes is hereby prohibited.

Section 2. The Congress and the several States shall have concurrent power to enforce this article by appropriate legislation.

Section 3. This article shall be inoperative unless it shall have been ratified as an amendment to the Constitution by the legislatures of the several States, as provided in the Constitution, within seven years from the date of the submission hereof to the States by the Congress.

Amendment XIX   The right of citizens of the United States to vote shall not be denied or abridged by the United States or by any State on account of sex.

Congress shall have power to enforce this article by appropriate legislation.

Amendment XX   *Section 1.* The terms of the President and Vice President shall end at noon on the 20th day of January, and the terms of Senators and Representatives at noon on the 3d day of January, of the years in which such terms would have ended if this article had not been ratified; and the terms of their successors shall then begin.

Section 2. The Congress shall assemble at least once in every year, and such meeting shall begin at noon on the 3d day of January, unless they shall by law appoint a different day.

Section 3. If, at the time fixed for the beginning of the term of the President, the President elect shall have died, the Vice President elect shall become President. If a President shall not have been chosen before the time fixed for the beginning of his term, or if the President elect shall have failed to qualify, then the Vice President elect shall act as President until a President shall have qualified; and the Congress may by law provide for the case wherein neither a President elect nor a Vice President elect shall have qualified, declaring who shall then act as President, or the manner in which one who is to act shall be selected, and such person shall act accordingly until a President or Vice President shall have qualified.

Section 4. The Congress may by law provide for the case of the death of any of the persons from whom the House of Representatives may choose a President whenever the right of choice shall have devolved upon them, and for the case of the death of any of the persons from whom the Senate may choose a Vice President whenever the right of choice shall have devolved upon them.

Section 5. Sections 1 and 2 shall take effect on the 15th day of October following the ratification of this article.

Section 6. This article shall be inoperative unless it shall have been ratified as an amendment to the Constitution by the legislatures of three-fourths of the several States within seven years from the date of its submission.

Amendment XXI   *Section 1.* The eighteenth article of amendment to the Constitution of the United States is hereby repealed.

Section 2. The transportation or importation into any State, Territory, or possession of the United States for delivery or use therein of intoxicating liquors, in violation of the laws thereof, is hereby prohibited.

Section 3. This article shall be inoperative unless it shall have been ratified as an amendment to the Constitution by conventions in the several States, as provided in the Constitution, within seven years from the date of the submission hereof to the States by the Congress.

Amendment XXII   *Section 1.* No person shall be elected to the office of the President more than twice, and no person who has held the office of President, or acted as President, for more than two years of a term to which some other person was elected President shall be elected to the office of the President more than once. But this Article shall not apply to any person holding the office of the President when this Article was proposed by the Congress, and shall not prevent any person who may be holding the office of President, or acting as President, during the term within which this Article becomes operative from holding the office of President or acting as President during the remainder of such term.

Section 2. This article shall be inoperative unless it shall have been ratified as an amendment to the Constitution by the legislatures of three-fourths of the several States within seven years from the date of its submission to the States by the Congress.

Amendment XXIII   *Section 1.* The District constituting the seat of Government of the United States shall appoint in such manner as the Congress may direct:

A number of electors of President and Vice President equal to the whole number of Senators and Representatives in Congress to which the District would be entitled if it were a State, but in no event more than the least populous State; they shall be in addition to those appointed by the States, but they shall be considered, for the purposes of the election of President and Vice President, to be electors appointed by a State; and they shall meet in the District and perform such duties as provided by the twelfth article of amendment.

Section 2. The Congress shall have power to enforce this article by appropriate legislation.

Amendment XXIV

Section 1. The right of citizens of the United States to vote in any primary or other election for President or Vice President, for electors for President or Vice President, or for Senator or Representative in Congress, shall not be denied or abridged by the United States or any State by reason of failure to pay any poll tax or other tax.

Section 2. The Congress shall have power to enforce this article by appropriate legislation.

Amendment XXV

Section 1. In case of the removal of the President from office or of his death or resignation, the Vice President shall become President.

Section 2. Whenever there is a vacancy in the office of the Vice President, the President shall nominate a Vice President who shall take office upon confirmation by a majority vote of both Houses of Congress.

Section 3. Whenever the President transmits to the President pro tempore of the Senate and the Speaker of the House of Representatives his written declaration that he is unable to discharge the powers and duties of his office, and until he transmits to them a written declaration to the contrary, such powers and duties shall be discharged by the Vice President as Acting President.

Section 4. Whenever the Vice President and a majority of either the principal officers of the executive departments or of such other body as Congress may by law provide, transmit to the President pro tempore of the Senate and the Speaker of the House of Representatives their written declaration that the President is unable to discharge the powers and duties of his office, the Vice President shall immediately assume the powers and duties of the office as Acting President.

Thereafter, when the President transmits to the President pro tempore of the Senate and the Speaker of the House of Representatives his written declaration that no inability exists, he shall resume the powers and duties of his office unless the Vice President and a majority of either the principal officers of the executive department or of such other body as Congress may by law provide, transmit within four days to the President pro tempore of the Senate and the Speaker of the House of Representatives their written declaration that the President is unable to discharge the powers and duties of his office. Thereupon Congress shall decide the issue, assembling within forty-eight hours for that purpose if not in session. If the Congress, within twenty-one days after receipt of the latter written declaration, or, if Congress is not in session, within twenty-one days after Congress is required to assemble, determines by two-thirds vote of both Houses that the President is unable to discharge the powers and duties of his office, the Vice President shall continue to discharge the same as Acting President; otherwise, the President shall resume the powers and duties of his office.

Amendment XXVI

Section 1. The right of citizens of the United States, who are eighteen years of age or older, to vote shall not be denied or abridged by the United States or by any State on account of age.

Section 2. The Congress shall have power to enforce this article by appropriate legislation.

Amendment XXVII

No law varying the compensation for the services of the Senators and Representatives, shall take effect, until an election of Representatives shall have intervened.

APPENDIXES

Appendix A
Locations of the Amendments in the Modern Edition of the Constitution

The Bill of Rights

The first ten amendments to the Constitution, commonly called the Bill of Rights, are set forth in the following clauses of the Modern Edition.

AMENDMENT	SUBJECT	CLAUSES
1	No law respecting an establishment of religion, or prohibiting the free exercise thereof	5.6
	Freedom of speech and the press	5.7
	Right to assemble and petition	5.8
2	Right to keep and bear arms	5.10
3	Limitation on quartering soldiers in houses	5.22
4	Freedom from unreasonable searches and seizures	5.11
5	Indictment or presentment by grand jury	5.24, 7.39
	Ban on double jeopardy	5.14
	Ban on compelling testimony against oneself	5.12
	Right to due process of law	5.1
	Just compensation for private property taken	5.9

AMENDMENT	SUBJECT	CLAUSES
6	Right to trial by jury and assistance of counsel in criminal cases	5.15
	Location of trial, jury of the state and district	5.25
	Right to be informed of accusation	5.16
	Right to confront witnesses, right to have compulsory process	5.17
7	Suits at common law: right to trial by jury, rules of the common law	1.72, 5.21, 7.38
8	Ban on excessive bail and fines, and cruel and unusual punishments	5.18, 5.19
9	Rights retained by the people	5.20
10	Powers reserved to the states or to the people	3.15

The Later Amendments

The amendments adopted after the Bill of Rights are set forth in the following clauses of the Modern Edition.

11	Ban on exercise of the judicial power in suits of persons against states	2.44
12	Election of President and Vice President	1.22, 1.26, 1.28–1.32, 7.29
13	Abolition of slavery	5.3
14	Citizenship, due process, equal protection, results of the Civil War	1.3, 2.7, 4.1, 5.1–5.2, 5.29, 7.14–7.16, 7.19–7.20
15	Right of all races to vote	4.2, 4.6, 7.13
16	Power to tax incomes	2.6
17	Election of senators by the people	1.7, 1.10, 7.24, 7.36
18	Prohibition of the manufacture, sale, transportation, importation, and exportation of intoxicating liquors	7.45, 8.2–8.3
19	Right of women to vote	4.3, 4.6

Appendix B
Editing the Constitution

Typographical Errors in the Constitution Corrected in the Modern Edition

A Surplus *S*

The 17th Amendment, section 1:

"qualifications requisite for electors of the state legislatures"

is corrected in the Modern Edition, Clause 1.7:

"qualifications requisite for electors of the state legislature."

The surplus *s* appeared in the amendment as introduced, and was removed after discussion of it by actions of both the House of Representatives (April 13, 1911) and the Senate (May 23, 1911). The two houses approved differing amendments, which were sent to a conference committee (a committee composed of members of the two houses).

The *s* reappeared in the language agreed upon by the conference committee, which was adopted by both houses without further discussion of the *s*; the proposed amendment was sent to the states for ratification on May 13, 1912.

A Missing *S*

The 25th Amendment, section 4, clause 2:

"principal officers of the executive department"

is corrected in the Modern Edition, Clause 1.46:

"principal officers of the executive departments."

The necessary *s* was present in all of the versions of the amendment that were considered by the Senate and House of Representatives, and in the two differing amendments that they approved.

The *s* disappeared in the language agreed upon by the conference committee, which was adopted by both houses without discussion of the *s*; the proposed amendment was sent to the states for ratification on July 6, 1965.

Comment

While such errors are often called typographical, these appear to have been committed, not by the printers but by the typists, proof readers, legal advisers, and indeed by the members, of Congress.

About the Editor

THE MODERN EDITION OF THE CONSTITUTION was produced by Henry Bain. A political scientist, he graduated from Swarthmore College and received his Ph.D. degree from Harvard University. He has had a long career in governmental research and consulting, and has taught at several universities.

Dr. Bain's early research on voting behavior included the first study to produce statistically significant evidence that voters tend to favor the first candidate on the list. His expert testimony in a California courtroom led that state's supreme court to rule the incumbents-first ballot law unconstitutional.

He participated in the planning of the rapid transit systems of San Francisco (BART) and Washington, D.C. (Metrorail). He was also a member of the team of social scientists who advised on the planning of the new city of Columbia, Maryland.

Dr. Bain is at work on a scholarly and critical study of the manner in which the original Constitution was written and printed, and of the many forms in which the constitutional text has been printed since 1787.

INDEX

Index to the Modern Edition of the Constitution

The numbers refer to chapters and clauses of the Modern Edition, **P** refers to the Preamble, and **n** means footnote. Subheadings for the three branches of the national government, under which appear their OFFICES, POWERS, and PROCEDURES, are shown in small capitals.

Users of the Index should bear in mind that numbers beginning with **7** refer to The Constitution of the Past. This part of the document no longer has any effect.